Berlitz®

Paris

Berlitz®
Paris

Text by Martin Gostelow
Revised by Alan Brent Gregston
Photography: Jay Fechtman except pages 9, 26, 46, 49, 70, 72, 76, 79, 82, 95 by Pete Bennett
Cover photograph by Jay Fechtman
Photo Editor: Naomi Zinn
Cartography by Raffaele Degennaro

Twelfth Edition 2002

CONTACTING THE EDITORS
Every effort has been made to provide accurate information in this publication, but changes are inevitable. The publisher cannot be responsible for any resulting loss, inconvenience or injury. We would appreciate it if readers would call our attention to any errors or outdated information by contacting Berlitz Publishing, PO Box 7910, London SE1 1WE, England.
Fax: (44) 20 7403 0290;
e-mail: berlitz@apaguide.demon.co.uk

Printed in Singapore by Insight Print Services (Pte) Ltd, 38 Joo Koon Road, Singapore 628990. Tel: (65) 6865-1600. Fax: (65) 6861-6438
Berlitz Trademark Reg. U.S. Patent Office and other countries. Marca Registrada
ISBN 2-8315-7703-9   040/212 REV

CONTENTS

● A (☞) in the text denotes a highly recommended sight

Paris

PARIS AND
THE PARISIANS

A place as full of life and movement as Paris defies its clichés faster than you can coin them. In a city fashioned by life around the River Seine (its main artery), is the Left Bank still the home of artists and intellectuals? Yes and no. The big publishers are still there, the Académie Française and the University of the Sorbonne, too, but many of the major fashion houses have now moved in on the little art galleries and bookshops.

Does the Right Bank remain the stronghold of the bourgeoisie? Yes and no. The grandest hotels and the most luxurious shops and department stores are still there, along with the embassies near the president's palace. But artists and writers increasingly occupy the Right Bank's new galleries and studio-lofts, and literary cafés have mushroomed around the old Bastille area and the Beaubourg quarter surrounding the Centre Georges Pompidou cultural complex.

The creative types have brought with them their avant garde theatre (once a Left Bank prerogative) and have spiced up the Right Bank's traditional preference for middle-class *boulevard* comedy. Other artists have preferred to stay in their time-honoured haunts on the periphery, around Montmartre in the north, where tourists still have their portraits done on the place du Tertre, or in Montparnasse in the south, in the more remote back streets away from the busy boulevards.

Several of the bridges linking the two riverbanks – the old Pont Neuf, the new Pont des Arts boardwalk, and the gilded Pont Alexandre III – continue as romantic rendezvous sites for lovers. So, yes, Paris is still a town for broken hearts, a place to come to mend one, or to break one you thought was safely whole. But it is also a surprisingly efficient town, with superb public transport and an abundance of pharmacies, cafés, bakeries, and markets, all of which combine to give the tourist a feeling of being at least a temporary resident. And just when people began lamenting the onslaught of fast-food outlets which drove many old bistros out of business, a new generation of young chefs has reinvigorated the restaurant scene with fresh takes on traditional French food.

As for another common misapprehension, the belief that Paris is very expensive, it's important to note that the best show in town comes absolutely free: the street life. Stroll along a quiet back street among the antiques shops and galleries of St-Germain-des-Prés, or perhaps across a leafy square in the old Marais quarter, or along a noisy boulevard

The Name Game

Visitors arriving in Paris by air imagine, understandably, that the airport they are flying into is named Charles-de-Gaulle, as written on their ticket. Then, they hear Parisians talking about "Roissy" and wonder where that is. It is, of course, the same place, the suburban location of the airport. Very few Parisians even know that the place de l'Etoile, at the top of the Champs-Elysées, should in fact be known as place Charles de Gaulle. The Centre Georges Pompidou, named after De Gaulle's successor, is known to almost all Parisians simply as "Beaubourg", the cultural centre's neighbourhood. The new Bibliothèque François Mitterrand is more commonly known as the Bibliothèque Nationale de France (National Library of France) or, in a word-play allusion to the TGV express train, as TGB (Très Grande Bibliothèque). Parisians are perfectly happy to vote for someone as president. They just don't seem to want to name something important after him.

Spend a morning in search of an undiscovered masterpiece at one of many artist stalls on the place du Tertre.

near the elegant old Opéra Garnier, and help yourself to a day-long feast for all five senses.

To please the eye, like any good theatre, Paris has its set-pieces, with broad avenues and esplanades deliberately laid out in the 19th century to create the perfect view of the Arc de Triomphe, the domes of the Panthéon and the Invalides, or that gloriously brazen monument, the Tour Eiffel. Among the many more recent buildings worth seeing are the splendid Pyramid at the Louvre, the more controversial Centre Georges Pompidou, and the new Bibliothèque Nationale opposite the American Cultural Centre (now converted into the French Cinémathèque).

Paris spends a fortune on illuminating major buildings after dark, enhancing its reputation as the City of Light. In fact, it already earns the name in the daytime, thanks to the interplay of sun, river, and predominantly white or honey-coloured stone facades. The peculiarly "Mediterranean" effect of this northern city has of course been immortalised by the Impressionists. In the morning a silver-and-blue light is cast over the shimmering Seine. In the afternoon, a soft glow bathes the vast place de la Concorde and handsome mansions on the Ile St-Louis.

And the smells… An early morning walk may take you past the basement window of a bakerery wafting the aroma of fresh baguette loaves. Or it may lead to a less seductive confrontation with a huge side of beef being shouldered past a row of rabbits, pheasants and poultry hanging in a butcher's shop window. The *bon vivant* thinks of a great *entrecôte* steak or roast duck for dinner and walks on to the flower market on the Ile de la Cité.

The Pont d'Léna, one of more than 30 bridges that span the Seine, each with its own beauty and style.

Then there are the sounds. Under the trees on the elongated triangle of place Dauphine, a lone accordionist (back in fashion now) may be playing an upbeat version of *Autumn Leaves* outside the house where the song's best-loved French interpreter, Yves Montand, used to live. For the other senses, there are those bridges.

And when you stop at a café terrace on the Champs-Elysées, think of the price of a cup of coffee – true, it *is* steep – as the cost of renting a table and ringside seat on one of the finest avenues of the Western world. People-watching here is a major sport.

Are the people of Paris really as arrogant as they are reputed to be? Or is it fairer to say they have much to be arrogant about? They have a beautiful city and they know it. They complain about it, too, much more than any irritated foreigner might, but usually because they believe they deserve the best and demand it. In fact, the character of many Parisians is as complex as their city's architecture. They are outwardly formidable, sometimes as bombastic as some of their historic monuments on the great squares and broad avenues, but they are also witty, stylish and charmingly accessible in their personal dealings.

Contrary to popular myth, Parisian women are not in fact more beautiful or prettier than elsewhere, but their self-confidence enables them to take the same T-shirt, jacket, jeans and scarf that can be bought anywhere nowadays and put them together in such a manner that they just end up looking better. The effect is reinforced by the similarly self-confident way they sit, stand or walk along the boulevard.

Ultimately, however, there is no "Parisian" type. The population of just over 2 million comes from all over France – Brittany, Normandy, Provence, Burgundy, Picardy or Corsica. The Parisians' traditional contempt for the "provinces" is matched only by their fierce regional loyalty to the distant home of their ancestors, often just one or two generations removed, and regularly revisited during the summer holiday season.

Despite recent attempts at "decentralisation", Paris continues to dominate French art, literature, music, fashion, education, scientific research, commerce and politics. The city is also a showcase for the many distinctive culinary traditions of France. This gives newcomers to France the advantage of sampling each of the country's regional cuisines without ever having to leave the capital. Often you will find a region's restaurants clustered around the railway station serving that particular area. For example, there is a large number of Breton restaurants and *crêperies* around the Gare Montparnasse, for that is where yesterday's "provincials" stopped off and set up home as Parisians.

Two French expressions that need no translation: *savoir faire* and *joie de vivre*.

Immigration and globalisation have also helped create a more interesting range of restaurants in recent years. There are now many very good North African, Vietnamese, Thai, Chinese and Japanese, as well as less impressive Indian and Italian establishments, among the city's nearly 12,000 bistros and restaurants.

Shopping remains one of the great Paris adventures, but don't expect to find any amazing bargains. This city has been around long enough to learn the correct price for everything, whether the object of your desire is in a place Vendôme jewellery store, a rue Jacob antique shop, a St-Ouen flea market, or a boulevard St-Michel souvenir stand. Nightlife, whether it be the theatre, the opera, a concert, a vaudeville or cabaret show, a disco or a nightclub, is certainly not cheap, but it is extremely vibrant and worth a splurge for a special memory of this incorrigibly festive city.

A BRIEF HISTORY

Beginnings

Paris began as a small fishing community and trading port in the middle of the River Seine. Stone Age inhabitants left the earliest traces (3000 BC) on the Right Bank under what is now the Musée du Louvre, along with remains of canoes which were recently uncovered while foundations were being laid for the new Finance Ministry. It was around 250 BC that the town took form under the skilful hands of the Parisii, a Celtic tribe that settled on the Ile de la Cité. Their island, well away from the banks of a river much wider and more swiftly flowing than today, provided refuge from the fierce Belgae to the east. The Parisii minted their own finely crafted gold coins for trade as far afield as Britain and the Mediterranean. The town's prosperity and strategic position at a crossroads of waterways attracted the attention of Julius Caesar's Roman legions, who conquered it in 52 BC.

Land immediately bordering the river was too marshy – the town's ancient name of Lutetia means "marshland" – so the Romans extended the town further inland on the Left Bank to what is now the Latin Quarter. Rue St-Jacques, prolonged to the north as rue St-Martin, traces the route of the Romans' characteristically straight road linking northern France to Orléans. Only scant subterranean masonry has been found from most of their buildings – forum, theatres, temples – but substantial remains of the monumental public baths (2nd and 3rd centuries AD) today form a wing of the Cluny Museum of Medieval Art.

St Denis brought Christianity to the city around AD 250 and was promptly decapitated by the Romans on the hill of Montmartre. According to legend, the martyr picked up his head and walked away with it tucked under his arm.

Overrunning Roman Gaul in the late 3rd century, Huns and Franks drove Lutetia's citizens to retrench in the fortified Ile de la Cité. The town changed its name to Paris; in 508, Clovis, king of the Franks, set up his court in what is today the Palais de Justice. He converted to Christianity, and several religious foundations date from this time – among them the earliest church in Paris, St-Germain-des-Prés.

Good Times and Bad

From 845 on, Norman pirates regularly raided Paris. The city stagnated until Hugues Capet, Count of Paris, became King of France in 987. His Capetian dynasty would make the city France's economic and political capital. The River Seine was once again the key to commercial prosperity, symbolised by the ship on the city's coat of arms with the

motto, *Fluctuat nec mergitur* (It floats but doesn't sink). The Right Bank port area, known as the Grève, grew up around the present-day Hôtel de Ville. (The French for "on strike", *en grève* derives from this traditional meeting place for striking port workers.)

Philippe Auguste (1180–1223) used the revenues from river trade to build Notre-Dame, a fortress named the

Statue of the triumphant Charlemagne overlooking the Ile de la Cité.

Louvre (its lower ramparts are clearly visible beneath the museum), as well as paved streets, aqueducts and fresh-water fountains. To protect his investment while he was away on the Third Crusade, he surrounded the city with walls.

Louis IX (1226–1270) gave the city one of its great Gothic masterpieces, the Sainte-Chapelle, and his patronage of spiritual and intellectual life created the Left Bank's Latin Quarter. From the many new schools frequented by Latin-speaking clerics, a university evolved under the name of the foremost college, La Sorbonne, established by the king's chaplain, Robert de Sorbon. By the end of Louis' reign, a population of 100,000 had made Paris one of the largest cities in Western Christendom.

In the 14th century, the city's merchant class took advantage of the political vacuum left by the devastating Black Death and the Hundred Years' War with England. With King Jean le Bon held prisoner at Poitiers in 1356, the merchants' leader, Etienne Marcel, set up a municipal government in Paris. Although he was assassinated two years' later, Marcel had shown that the Parisians were a force to be reckoned with. Wary of their militancy, Jean's successor, Charles V, constructed the Bastille fortress.

Civil unrest continued unabated. In 1407, the Duke of Burgundy had the Duke of Orléans murdered on the rue Barbette, leading to 12 years of strife between their supporters. The Burgundians called in the help of the English, who entered Paris in 1420.

Ten years' later, Joan of Arc tried and failed to get them out again, and in the following year came a worse humiliation: England's Henry VI was crowned King of France in Notre-Dame cathedral in Paris. However, the English triumph was short-lived. They were soon expelled from the city, and by 1453 had lost all their French possessions except for Calais.

Paris Becomes Paris

With François I (1515–47), the city learnt to thrive under an absolutist and absent monarch who was busy with wars in Italy and even a year's imprisonment in Spain. Much of the Louvre was torn down and rebuilt along the present lines. A new Hôtel de Ville (city hall) was begun, as well as the splendid Saint-Eustache church.

Parisians were already assuming that distinctive pride in the uniqueness of their city. The poet François Villon sang: *"Il n'y a bon bec que de Paris"* (Only Parisians have real wit), while Pierre de Ronsard saw Paris as "the city imbued with the discipline and glory of the muses."

Discipline and glory soon drowned in the blood of religious war. It started in 1572 with the infamous St Bartholomew's Day massacre of 3,000 Protestants in Paris and culminated in the siege of the city by Henri de Navarre in 1589. Before the Catholic League capitulated, 13,000 Parisians had died of starvation. Henri was crowned at Chartres and finally entered the capital in 1594 – but not before he had turned Catholic himself, with the notorious quip that "Paris is well worth a Mass."

Henri IV did Paris proud once he was its master. He built the beautiful place des Vosges and place Dauphine, embellished the banks of the river with the quais de l'Arsenal, de l'Horloge and des Orfèvres, and even constructed the Samaritaine hydraulic machine that pumped fresh water to Right Bank households up until 1813. The most popular of France's monarchs, *le bon roi Henri* (good King Henry) was a notorious ladies' man. He completed the Pont-Neuf (the oldest bridge in Paris) as well as the adjacent gardens, where he was known to dally with his ladies.

During the reign of Louis XIII (1610–43), Paris began to take on the fashionable aspect that became its hallmark.

Elegant houses sprang up along the rue du Faubourg-St-Honoré, and the magnificent *hôtels* (mansions) of the nobility mushroomed in the Marais. The capital strengthened its hold on the country with the establishment of a royal printing press, the Académie Française of Cardinal Richelieu, and in gaining ecclesiastical status as an archbishopric.

Paris increasingly attracted nobles from the provinces – too many for the liking of Louis XIV, *le roi Soleil* (the Sun King, 1643–1715). To bring his overly powerful and independent aristocrats back into line, Louis decided to move the court out to Versailles, compelling the courtiers to live at ruinous expense in his enormous new palace.

Paris lost its political importance, but looked more impressive than ever with the landscaping of the Jardin des Tuileries and the Champs-Elysées, and the construction of the Louvre's

With its combination of late-Gothic design and Renaissance detail, the Saint-Eustache church continues to impress visitors.

great colonnade and the Invalides hospital for wounded soldiers. The city asserted a leading cultural position in Europe with its new academies of the arts, literature and sciences and the establishment of the Comédie Française (1680) and several other theatres. The population had increased to 560,000.

The rumble of popular discontent grew louder as corruption and heavy taxes for costly foreign wars marked the reigns of the Sun King's successors, the languid Louis XV (1715–74) and the inept Louis XVI. One of the final construction projects of the *ancien régime* was a 23-km (14-mile) wall encircling the city. Begun in 1784, this became a major factor in the subsequent unrest, for it was at points along the wall that taxes were collected on the various goods brought into the city.

Revolution and After

Seizing power from the royal court at Versailles, Paris became the epicentre for the political earthquake of the French Revolution, whose aftershocks spread across France to shake up a whole continent. It had all started with protests about taxes and turned into an assault on the privileges of the monarchy, the aristocracy and the church. Middle-class intellectuals made common cause with the urban poor, the previously powerless *sans-culottes* (literally, people without breeches) to revolt.

The revolutionaries carted away the masonry of the prison-fortress of the Bastille destroyed on 14 July 1789 to build the bridge leading to what was then the place de la Révolution – now the place de la Concorde. There, the remarkably efficient guillotine was erected to execute the perceived enemies of the new republic.

A climax was reached on 21 January 1793, with the public beheading of Louis XVI. In the Reign of Terror later that year, several revolutionaries followed Louis to the guillotine: Camille Desmoulins, the fiery orator; Danton, who tried to moderate the Terror; and then the men who had organised it, Robespierre and Saint-Just.

In 1799, Napoléon Bonaparte became dictator and later emperor. For Paris itself, he performed all the functions of an enthusiastic mayor, scarcely hindered by his military expeditions abroad. In Moscow, for instance, he found time to draw up statutes for the Comédie Française. Detailed maps of the city and architectural plans for new buildings were always part of his baggage. Despite his spectacular monuments of the Arc de Triomphe and the column of the Grande-Armée on the Place Vendôme, the emperor was proudest of his civic improvements: better fresh water supplies throughout the city, improved drainage, new food markets and a streamlined municipal administration and police force. The majority of his reforms survived long after his fall in 1814 and final defeat the following year. Taken as a whole, his civic achievements became a model for modern urban government.

The monarchy returned, but faced an ever-present threat in Paris from dissatisfied workers, radical intellectuals and an ambitious bourgeoisie. In July 1830, protest turned to riots and the building of barricades. Charles X was forced to abdicate. But instead of restoring the republic, the revolutionary leaders played it safe and accepted the moderate Louis-Philippe or "Citizen King".

The Revolution of 1848, which brought Louis-Philippe's monarchy to an end, likewise started with riots and barricades in the streets of Paris. A mob threatened the royal palace, forcing the king to flee, and then invaded the Chamber of Deputies, demanding a republic. Elections followed, but they showed that, however radical Paris might be, the rest of France was still largely conservative. The new National Assembly withdrew the

Built in the early 17th century, the Palais du Luxembourg now houses the French Senate.

concessions that had been made to the workers, and up went the barricades again. This time the army was called in with its heavy guns. At least 1,500 insurrectionists were killed, and thousands deported. The democratically elected president, Louis-Napoléon, seized absolute power in 1851 and the following year became Emperor Napoléon III. (He was a nephew of Napoléon Bonaparte, whose son and second-in-line died young without ever having reigned.)

Fear led Napoléon III to modernise Paris. The insurrections of 1830 and 1848 had flared up in the densely populated working-class districts around the centre, and he wanted to prevent any chance of a recurrence. He commissioned Baron Georges Haussmann to do away with the narrow alleys that nurtured discontent. The baron moved the occupants out to the suburbs, creating the "red belt", which makes Paris one of the few Western capitals with suburbs that are not predominantly conservative.

The city was opened up with broad boulevards and avenues, giving Paris its modern airy look and highlighting the main monuments, churches and public buildings. As the baron explained to his emperor, these avenues were too wide for barricades and gave the artillery a clear line of fire in case of revolt.

This Second Empire was also a time of joyous abandon and boisterous expansion. The composer Jacques Offenbach's operettas epitomise this period. But the emperor stumbled into war against Prussia in 1870. The army was quickly defeated and Napoleon III's disgrace and capture brought the proclamation of a new republic, followed by a crippling Prussian siege of Paris. The city held out, though reduced to starvation level.

When France's leaders agreed to peace, there was yet another uprising. The Paris Commune (self-rule by the workers) lasted 10 weeks, from 18 March to 29 May 1871, until Adolphe Thiers, the first president of the Third Republic, sent in troops from Versailles to crush it. In the last days, the *communards* set fire to the Palais des Tuileries and executed hostages, including the Archbishop of Paris. The government took its vengeance: at least 20,000 Commune supporters were killed in the fighting or were executed afterwards.

Peace and War

Prosperity rapidly returned, marked by a great construction boom. Projects begun under Napoléon III, such as the Opéra Garnier and the huge Les Halles market, were completed. The city showed off its new face at the 1889 world's fair, with the Tour Eiffel as its grandiose symbol. The splendid *métro* subway system was inaugurated in 1900.

In the same year, Picasso came over from Barcelona, one of many artists, writers and revolutionaries flocking to this hub of creative activity. He was followed by Modigliani from Livorno, Soutine from Minsk, and Stravinsky and Trotsky from St Petersburg. Gertrude Stein, Man Ray, Ernest Hemingway and F. Scott Fitzgerald led the American "colony".

Two wars, of course, took their toll. The Germans failed to take Paris during World War I, but they occupied it for four long and unhappy years (1940–44) during World War II. Unlike many European capitals, Paris escaped large-scale bombing and Hitler's vengeful order to destroy the city before retreating was ignored. Liberation came eventually, with a parade down the Champs-Elysées by General Charles de Gaulle, his Free French forces and American and British allies.

The post-war city regained some of its cultural lustre when the existential philosopher Jean-Paul Sartre held court in St-Germain-des-Prés, but under a rapid succession of governments, economic recovery was slow. The Fourth Republic died, without regrets, in 1958, after an army revolt during the colonial war in Algeria. Recalled from retirement, General de Gaulle became the first president of the Fifth Republic and set about restoring French prestige and morale.

Recent Times

Barricades and insurrection returned to Paris in May 1968. With workers on strike, students hurled the Latin Quarter's paving stones at the smug Establishment. But national elections showed that Paris was once more at odds with most of France, which voted for stability. Succeeding de Gaulle, Georges Pompidou affirmed the new prosperity with controversial riverside expressways and skyscrapers, and the visually striking Beaubourg cultural centre that bears his name.

In 1977, Jacques Chirac became the first democratically elected mayor of Paris in over a century. At a time when politicians could double as mayor and prime minister, Parisians benefited from leaders who furthered their national political ambitions with a dynamic municipal performance. While many questioned his taste in the shopping mall that replaced the old markets of Les Halles, Chirac is credited with the effective clean-up of the formerly dirty streets.

As president, François Mitterrand made his own mark on the Paris skyline with a series of imposing works: the great

Napoléon ordered the cannons of the Musée de l'Armée to be fired on great occasions, including the birth of his son in 1811.

Pyramid that highlights the reorganised Louvre, the Grande Arche, the Opéra-Bastille, the Institut du Monde Arabe and the new national library that bears his name.

After a persistent 20-year campaign, Chirac moved from the mayor's job into that of president in 1995. Within two years, though, his popularity had fallen and Lionel Jospin, from the opposing Socialist Party, became prime minister. Their period of joint stewardship was one of economic growth, falling unemployment and rising property values in Paris. In the 2001 mayoral elections, Parisians elected Bertrand Delanoe, the city's first socialist mayor for 130 years and the first openly gay mayor in France. However, the first round of the 2002 presidential elections saw a massive resurgence of the right in which the National Front candidate Jean-Marie Le Pen beat Lionel Jospin. Though Jacques Chirac went on to beat Le Pen in the second round, the degree of support for Le Pen shocked governments all over Europe.

Historical Landmarks

ca. 250 BC Celtic settlement on island in the River Seine

52 BC Roman conquest, followed by expansion to Left Bank

508 Clovis, King of Franks, settles in Paris

987 Hugues Capet elected King of France

1163 Building of Notre-Dame cathedral begins

1420 The English occupy Paris

1431 Henry VI of England crowned King of France

1436 English expelled

1594 Henri IV enters Paris

1682 Louis XIV moves court to Versailles

1789 Storming of Bastille starts French Revolution

1793 Execution of Louis XVI and Marie Antoinette; Reign of Terror

1804 Napoléon becomes emperor

1814–15 Fall of Napoléon; restoration of Bourbon monarchy

1830 "Bourgeois revolution"; Louis-Philippe, the Citizen King

1848 Revolution brings Louis-Napoléon to power

1870–1 Franco-Prussian War; Second Empire ends; Paris besieged

1871 Paris Commune – 10 weeks of workers' rule

1900 First *Métro* line opened

1914–18 World War I

1939–45 World War II

1940 French government capitulates; Germans occupy Paris

1944 Free French and other Allied forces liberate Paris

1958 Fall of Fourth Republic; De Gaulle becomes president

1968 Student riots, workers' general strikes

1977 Jacques Chirac becomes first elected mayor since 1871

1981–95 President François Mitterrand's major new construction includes Louvre's Pyramid

1995 Jacques Chirac elected president

1998 New Bibliothèque Nationale inaugurated

2001 Bertrand Delanoe is Paris's first leftish mayor in 130 years

2002 Euro replaces franc as France's unit of currency

WHERE TO GO

GETTING AROUND

The first thing you should get is a *carnet*, or book of ten métro tickets (good for buses, too). Or, better still, if you're staying a week or more, one of the special passes which give even greater savings *(see page 118)*. Then, buy a Museum Pass *(see page 74)* to save money and avoid waiting at ticket counters.

To get your bearings, picture Paris as a circle, with the river Seine threading across the centre, flanked by famous landmarks – Notre-Dame, the Louvre, place de la Concorde, Arc de Triomphe, the Tour Eiffel. Bridges link the Right (north) and Left Banks via the two islands in the middle, the Ile de la Cité and Ile St-Louis.

This is one of the easiest of large cities to travel around. The modernised **métro** system is smooth, regular and fast, with low, flat-rate fares. RER commuter trains can also take you rapidly to the outskirts, where two major attractions, Versailles and the Disneyland Paris Resort, are located.

Buses give you a sightseeing tour at a bargain price, respecting schedules as far as traffic allows (rush hours can create terrible jams). **Taxis** provide a lazy alternative, but are not always faster than the métro, especially on longer rides across town.

Bus tours take you to the big attractions, but inevitably at times when they are busiest. Some tour buses that take you around the highlights let you hop on and off wherever and as often as you like, all on one ticket, for a period of up to 48 hours. Tourist information offices *(see page 122)* have details. **Bicycle** rental companies *(see page 103)* also run tours. If you want to sightsee in style (and expensively) you can even see Paris from a helicopter, plane, or hot-air balloon. **In-line skates** have become very popular for touring the town and can also be rented *(see page 103)*.

Parisians themselves often use the *Batobus* (river bus) for travelling east or west and avoiding traffic snarls (May–Sep only); stops are at the Tour Eiffel, Musée d'Orsay, Louvre, Notre-Dame and Hôtel de Ville. It's relatively expensive, but you may prefer the absence of commentary.

A **boat cruise** on the Seine is one of the best introductions to the city. While you glide along, multilingual commentaries tell you about the sights. Boats run from about 10am–10.30pm. Most tour boats provide a choice of open-air and glassed-in seating; some offer lunch and dinner. Trips last 60–75 minutes. **Canal tours** reveal a less grand but more intimate face of Paris on the way from the centre to Parc de la Villette *(see page 72)* in the northeastern outskirts. The leisurely trip takes three hours, with a tunnel and several locks to be negotiated.

Central Paris is surprisingly compact, and most hotels are close to many of the sights. So if time isn't a major factor, the

Summer breeze, soft shade and the gentle current of the Seine at place du Vert Galant on the Ile de la Cité.

best way of getting the feel of the place is to **walk**. All you need is a pair of comfortable shoes and a **map**. The big department stores and hotels give away millions of street maps each year. Métro stations display good maps of their local district as well as the métro itself, and give out pocket plans of the métro and bus routes. At street level, bus-stop shelters have an excellent detailed map of the neighbourhood. More and more streets and entire areas like Les Halles and Beaubourg have been pedestrianised, adding to the profusion of parks, squares and gardens.

THE ISLANDS

Ile de la Cité

This is where the city's story began. Like the emblem on its coat of arms, the Ile de la Cité takes the form of a boat, with the romantic tree-shaded **place du Vert Galant** as its prow pointing downstream. From the first settlement built by the original Parisii until the middle of the 19th century, the pocket-sized island lay at the heart of the city. The earliest rulers held court here. The cathedral clergy and artisans made it their home. Then, ruthless urban planner Baron Haussmann swept away almost all the medieval and 17th-century structures, leaving just place Dauphine and rue Chanoinesse (ancient home of the cathedral canons) as evidence of the island's once-rich residential life.

The baron was also considering the idea of replacing the gracious red-brick houses of the triangular **place Dauphine** with a neo-Grecian colonnaded square when he was forced out of office for financial irregularities. Near the lively **Pont-Neuf**, the *place* was built in 1607 by Henri IV in honour of his son the *dauphin* (or future king, Louis XIII). Sadly, only numbers 14 and 26 are still in their original state. Number 10 was the home of film stars Simone Signoret and Yves Montand.

The huge **Palais de Justice**, heart of the centralised French legal system, stands on the site of the Roman palace where the

Paris by Numbers

The city is divided into 20 districts or *arrondissements*, their numbers spiralling outwards, starting at the centre around the Louvre.

1er: The Louvre to Les Halles, half of Ile de la Cité

2e: South of the *grands boulevards*; financial district, theatres

3e: Quiet, old streets of the northern Marais

4e: Centre Georges-Pompidou to southern Marais; Jewish quarter; gay community

5e: Latin Quarter; educational institutions and student life

6e: St-Germain-des-Prés; intellectuals, bookshops, restaurants

7e: Musée d'Orsay to the Tour Eiffel; elegant apartments

8e: Champs-Elysées to Madeleine; luxury shops, fashion houses, mainstream cinemas

9e: Opéra-Garnier, theatres and big department stores

10e: Gare du Nord; North African and Asian neighbour-hoods; walks along Canal St-Martin

11e: Bastille; trendy galleries, nightlife; farther north, Oberkampf, the new "in" scene

12e: Bordering on the Bois de Vincennes; nearby zoo

13e: Tower blocks; large Asian community

14e: Montparnasse; commercial development, cinemas, cafés

15e: rue de Vaugirard (Paris' longest street); food markets

16e: Arc de Triomphe to Bois de Boulogne; expensive apartments and shops

17e: Chic residences; street market rue Lévis

18e: Montmartre and Pigalle; village life and low life

19e and 20e: Père Lachaise cemetery, Belleville; working-class quarters and La Villette

Emperor Julian was crowned in AD 360. Together with the Conciergerie *(see page 30)*, it sprawls right across the Ile de la Cité. Concealed in the courtyard between them is a Gothic masterpiece, the **Sainte-Chapelle**, the fine proportions of which stand in sharp contrast to the ponderous palace. The chapel *(see page 39)* was constructed in 1248 to house holy relics, fragments of what were believed to be Christ's Crown of Thorns and the True Cross, which pious Louis IX (later canonised as St Louis) had bought from the Byzantine emperor.

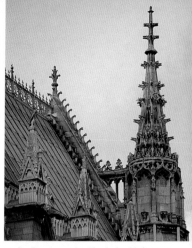

Gazing over the Ile de la Cité — the Gothic spires of the Sainte-Chapelle, built in 1248.

Try to arrive as the chapel opens or at sunset and make your way to the upper level, where light blazes through 15 stained-glass windows separated by buttresses so slim that there seems to be no wall at all. Miraculously, of the 1,134 individual pieces of glass, 720 are 13th-century originals. The chapel provides an exquisite setting for chamber music concerts.

Between 1789 and 1815 the chapel assumed various guises: a flour warehouse during the Revolution and a club for high-ranking dandies, then an archive for Napoléon's Consulate. It was this latter role that saved the chapel from projected destruction, since the bureaucrats could not think of another site in which to put their mountains of paper.

These days, they find room for their papers in the Palais de Justice and the nearby **Préfecture de Police**, haunt of those

The Pont-Neuf, the city's oldest bridge, is a popular place to meet and stroll.

fictional detectives, Inspectors Maigret and Clouseau. The great lobby of the Palais, the Salle des Pas Perdus, is worth a visit for a glimpse of the lawyers, plaintiffs, witnesses, court reporters and hangers-on waiting nervously for the wheels of French justice to grind into action.

Their anxiety is nothing compared with that of the prisoners once held in the forbidding **Conciergerie** (entrance on the quai de l'Horloge). It was originally the residence of the king's concierge as part of the 14th-century royal palace. In 1793, at the height of the Terror, it literally became the "antechamber of the guillotine". Queen Marie-Antoinette, Robespierre, Danton and Saint-Just all spent their last nights in the Galerie des Prisonniers. The Salle des Girondins displays a guillotine blade, the crucifix before which Marie-Antoinette prayed and the lock used on Robespierre's cell. Look out on the Cour des Femmes, where husbands, lovers, wives and mistresses were allowed one final tryst before the tumbrels came to carry off the condemned. About 2,500 victims of the Revolutionary guillotine spent their last hours in the Conciergerie.

Notre-Dame

The site of the cathedral of Notre-Dame de Paris has had a religious role for at least 2,000 years. In Roman times a temple to Jupiter stood here; some stone fragments unearthed in 1711 can be seen in the Musée du Moyen Age *(see page 55)*.

Bridges of Paris

Within the city, 36 bridges span the Seine. Whether you are walking or riding, there are some that you'll use frequently. Bridges also feature prominently on river cruises.

Pont-Neuf (new bridge) is in fact the oldest surviving bridge, dating from 1606 (the reign of Henri IV, who can be seen on horseback at the centre). It was kept free of the houses that lined earlier bridges, so it quickly became, and still is, a popular place to meet and stroll. Some of the hawkers, musicians and pickpockets who used to gather here are caricatured in grimacing stone heads on the cornice facing the river.

Pont des Arts is the next bridge downstream, a spidery iron structure reserved for walkers and a favourite meeting point on the way to the Latin Quarter.

Pont-Royal crosses where the Louvre meets the Tuileries Gardens. It was built for Louis XIV in 1685. The Passerelle Solférino Footbridge links the Right Bank Jardin des Tuileries to the Left Bank Musée d'Orsay.

Pont de la Concorde was built from stones taken from the Bastille. Its original name, Pont Louis XVI, was changed to Pont de la Révolution the year before the king went to the guillotine on nearby place de la Révolution (now place de la Concorde).

Pont Alexandre III was named after the Czar of Russia whose successor, Nicholas II, laid the first stone in 1896. It was the first bridge with a single steel arch. The cast-iron lamp standards are characteristic of the Belle Époque and gilded statues at the ends depict medieval and modern France (Right Bank) and Renaissance France and Louis XIV (Left Bank).

Pont de Bir-Hakeim, named after a celebrated World War II battle in the Libyan desert, is a railway viaduct for the Métro that provides travellers on the No. 6 line with a splendid view of the Tour Eiffel.

In the 4th century AD, the first Christian church, St-Etienne, was built, joined two centuries later by a second church, dedicated to Notre-Dame. Norman raids left both in a sorry state, and Bishop Maurice de Sully decided a cathedral should be built to replace them. Begun in 1163, the main part of Notre-Dame took 167 years to finish. Its transition from Romanesque to Gothic has been called a perfect representation of medieval architecture, an opinion that has ancient and modern dissenters. Cistercian monks protested that such a sumptuous structure was an insult to the godly virtue of poverty, and today architectural purists still find Notre-Dame a bit "too much". It was, however, built to inspire awe.

Over its long history, the cathedral has witnessed many momentous occasions. In 1239, there was the procession of Louis IX, barefoot, carrying his holy treasure, Christ's Crown of Thorns; in 1430, it saw the humiliation of Henry VI of England (he was crowned King of France here; *see page 15*). And in 1594, it was

where Henri IV made his politically motivated conversion to Catholicism, to reinforce his hold on the French throne. Napoléon crowned himself emperor here (upstaging the Pope, who had come to Paris expecting to do it).

In modern times, the cathedral has been a place for celebrating victory and mourning the passing of

The detailed facade of Notre-Dame cathedral – a long-time symbol of Paris.

France's leaders. General de Gaulle marked the 1944 Liberation of Paris with a Mass here, and in 1970 his death was similarly commemorated. In 1996, a funeral service was held for François Mitterrand.

Across the three doorways of the west front, the 28 statues of the **Galerie des Rois** represent the kings of Judah. These are 19th-century restorations: the originals were torn down during the Revolution because they were thought to depict kings of France (21 of them were recently discovered and preserved in the Musée du Moyen Age, *see page 55*). The superb central **rose window** depicts the Redemption after the Fall. Two more outsized rose windows illuminate the transept; the northern window retains most of its 13th-century glass. A lovely 14th-century **Virgin and Child**, emblematic of the cathedral's name, Notre-Dame de Paris (Our Lady of Paris), is to the right of the choir entrance.

The cathedral's original architect is unknown, but Pierre de Montreuil (who was involved in the building of Sainte-Chapelle) was responsible for a large part of the 13th-century work. The present state of the cathedral owes much to Eugène Viollet-le-Duc, who from 1845 to 1863 painstakingly restored it following the ravages of the 18th century, caused more by pre-Revolutionary meddlers than by revolutionaries who stripped it of religious symbols. Popular support for the costly restoration was inspired by Victor Hugo's novel, *The Hunchback of Notre-Dame*.

The 255-step climb up the **north tower** is rewarded with wonderful views of Paris and close-ups of the roof and gargoyles. Cross over to the south tower– and another 122 steps – to see the 13-ton bell, the only one remaining (the Revolutionaries melted down the others to make cannons). The bell was re-cast in the 1680s. A further 124 steps lead to the top of the south tower for other spectacular views.

Baron Haussmann greatly enlarged the *parvis*, the cathedral forecourt, diminishing the impact of the towering west front. Excavations beneath the square have revealed walls and foundations from the Gallic, Roman and medieval eras, which now form part of an exhibition on early Paris.

Ile St-Louis

The bridge across to Ile St-Louis leads to a blessed sanctuary of gracious living, its quiet streets lined by elegant houses and mansions. President Pompidou had a house on the quai de Béthune and used to escape there from the Elysée Palace as frequently as he could.

At 17 quai d'Anjou is the grand **Hôtel Lauzun**, built in the 1650s by Le Vau, who worked on the riverfront façade of the Louvre and the Versailles château. In the **Hôtel Lambert**, on the corner of the rue St-Louis-en-l'Ile, Voltaire once enjoyed a tempestuous love affair with the lady of the house, the Marquise du Châtelet. The airy, bright baroque church of **St-Louis-en-l'Ile** illuminates with a golden light its fine collection of Dutch, Flemish and Italian 16th- and 17th-century art.

From the western end of the shady quai d'Orléans there is a splendid view of the apse of Notre-Dame. However, other pilgrims to this spot are more intent on a visit to Berthillon, a hallowed maker of particularly good ice creams and refreshing sorbets.

RIGHT BANK

The sprawling Right Bank (*rive droite*) covers the whole range of Paris's social life, from ultra-chic to downright sleazy. It claims the most luxurious shopping areas, the presidential Elysée Palace, the grands boulevards and financial district, but also, further north, seamy Clichy and Pigalle, as well as hilly

The quiet streets, elegant houses, and courtly mansions of the Ile St-Louis have long been popular with the Parisian gentry.

Montmartre, where modern art could be said to have begun. Back in the middle of it all, the huge Louvre museum makes its own magnificent statement. Just to the east, Les Halles, Beaubourg (around the Centre Georges-Pompidou) and place de la Bastille have each been transformed by so-called *Grands Projets*. The variety and energy of the nightlife here has overtaken that of the Left Bank. The charming old Marais and its Jewish quarter, representing the old Paris of the 17th century, have taken on a new fashionable appearance with the influx of trendy boutiques.

Place Charles-de-Gaulle (l'Etoile)

Officially renamed place Charles de Gaulle after the death of De Gaulle in 1969, this is still known to Parisians as *l'Etoile* (the star) for the 12 avenues branching out from the centre like a star. The circular space with its whirling traffic is dominated by the **Arc de Triomphe**, 50 m (164 ft) high and 45 m (148 ft) wide. A trip to the top by lift affords spectacular views. It is here that you can best appreciate the

The massive Arc de Triomphe commemorates Napoléon's armies and their victories.

tour de force of geometric planning that the avenues represent.

Napoléon I conceived of the Arc de Triomphe as a tribute to his armies, and bears the names of hundreds of his marshals and generals, and dozens of victories. No defeats are recorded, naturally, although a few of the victories are debatable. Napoléon himself only ever saw a wood and canvas model: the arch was completed during the 1830s. It rapidly became the focus for state occasions, such as the return of the ex-emperor's own remains from St Helena in 1840 and for the funeral of Victor Hugo in 1885. In 1920, the Unknown Soldier of World War I was buried at the arch; three years later the eternal flame was lit. When Adolf Hitler arrived in Paris as a conqueror in 1940, the Arc de Triomphe was the first place he wanted to see. And at the Liberation, this was the spot where General de Gaulle commenced his triumphal march down the Champs-Elysées.

Avenue Foch, leading away from l'Etoile to the Bois de Boulogne, is one of the most majestic of the city's residential avenues. It is one of the most exclusive, too, though somewhat democratised these days by the groups of *boules* players on its gravelled side paths. Avenue de la Grande-Armée points straight to Neuilly and the towers of La Défense with the Grande Arche behind.

Avenue des Champs-Elysées

One of the finest avenues in the world, the Champs-Elysées slopes down to the place de la Concorde straight through a lovely parade of chestnut trees, the object of careful replanting to ensure that the avenue retains its elegant beauty.

The top two-thirds of the avenue are filled with cinemas, airline offices and car showrooms, the excellent **tourist information office** (No. 127) and café terraces that make perfect, if slightly expensive, vantage points for people-watching.

Below the Rond-Point, the mood changes and a pleasant park leads you past two landmarks: the **Petit Palais**, all steel and glass, and the **Grand Palais**. Both were constructed for the Universal Exhibition of 1900 and are today used for a variety of exhibitions, though the Petit Palais (closed for renovation until 2003) houses several permanent collections of 19th-century French paintings. The Grand Palais shares its colossal building with the Palais de la Découverte *(see page 75)* and includes among its displays a hands-on exhibition of the sciences, with a planetarium as centrepiece.

Jacques-Ange Gabriel designed the gigantic **place de la Concorde** as place Louis XV in 1753, but the Revolution dispensed with all royal connotations. A guillotine replaced the king's statue and was used to behead Louis XVI and more than 1,000 other victims. In 1934, it was the scene of bloody anti-government rioting by French fascists.

Topped by a gilded pyramidal tip, the 23-m (75-ft) pink granite **Obelisk** from the temple of Ramses II in Luxor dates back to 1300 BC and was erected here in 1836. For a change, it's not something that Napoléon looted during a campaign, but was a gift from Mohammed Ali, viceroy of Egypt. The two

The colossal Grand Palais, built in 1900, is still used to showcase a variety of exhibitions.

imposing horses guarding the entrance to the Champs-Elysées are replicas of the handsome 18th-century Chevaux de Marly, sculpted by Guillaume Coustou. (The marble originals now grace the Cour Marly of the Louvre.)

Jardin des Tuileries

The Jardin des Tuileries (named after a 13th-century tile works) has been beautifully re-landscaped based on the original plan of Le Nôtre, the landscape designer who created it for Louis XIV. Walk around the chestnut and lime trees, and admire Aristide Maillol's 18 sensual statues of nymphs and languorous maidens, a few of which are coquettishly half concealed behind a miniature maze.

The gardens' 28 hectares (11 acres) extend across the site of the royal Palais des Tuileries, burnt down during the 1871 Commune *(see page 21)*. A few fragments of the palace can be seen by the **Jeu de Paume** exhibition building, located in the northwest corner. Children can enjoy donkey rides, puppet shows in the spring and summer, and model boats on the

Paris Highlights

Arc de Triomphe. Monument commemorating Napoléon's armies and their victories. Open Apr–Sept 9.30am–11pm, Oct–Mar 10am–10.30pm (closes at 6.30pm Sun–Mon). Entrance free first Sunday of the month. Métro: Charles de Gaulle-Étoile.

Tour Eiffel. The world's tallest structure when it was built in 1889, and still a marvel. Open daily 9.30am–11pm, mid-June–31Aug 9am–midnight. Métro: Bir-Hakeim, École Militaire, Trocadéro.

La Défense. The Grande Arche is the high point (literally and figuratively) of this "little Manhattan". Grande Arche roof: open 9am–7pm (closes 8pm Sat, Sun and public holidays and at 6pm Oct–Mar). Métro: Grande Arche de la Défense.

Invalides. A 17th-century army veterans' hospital; home to the Army Museum and Napoléon's tomb. Open: Museum 10am–6pm (5pm Oct–Mar); Napoléon's tomb 10am–6pm (7pm Jun–Aug, 5pm Oct–Mar). Métro: Latour-Maubourg, Invalides.

La Madeleine. A neoclassical temple on the outside and an imposing church inside. Open Mon–Sat 7.30am–7pm; Sun 8am–1.30pm and 3.30–7pm. Métro: Madeleine.

Notre-Dame de Paris. Early Gothic masterpiece and the symbol of Paris for 800 years. The view from the towers is superb and the crypt reveals the Roman foundations of the city. Open 8am–6.45pm (Sat 8am–12.30pm and 2–7pm); Crypt 10am–6pm (5pm Oct–Mar). Métro: Cité, Cluny-La Sorbonne, Hôtel de Ville.

Sainte-Chapelle. A 13th-century jewel of Gothic architecture, with magnificent stained glass. Open 9.30am–6.30pm (10am–5pm Oct–Mar). Métro: Cité.

Place des Vosges. The heart of the Marais, Henri IV's harmoniously planned square of elegant 17th-century houses. Victor Hugo lived at No. 6, now a museum. Métro: St-Paul, Chemin-Vert.

circular ponds. Adults head for the giant Ferris wheel installed during the holiday season. In the corner near the Seine, facing place de la Concorde, the **Orangerie** (closed for renovation until 2003) is known for its two oval rooms with Monet's beautiful *Nymphéas* (Water Lilies) murals, but see, too, the excellent collection of Impressionist and post-Impressionist paintings upstairs *(see page 71)*.

At the eastern entrance to the Tuileries, the pink **Arc de Triomphe du Carrousel** was built at roughly the same time as its bigger brother at l'Etoile. The latter is visible from here in a straight line beyond the Obelisk on place de la Concorde. The same axis continues into the distant haze to the skyscrapers of La Défense and the Grande Arche.

Palais du Louvre

This is truly one of the world's treasure houses *(see page 67 for a description of its art collection)*. Despite being eight centuries in the making, it has preserved a wonderful harmony. First built as a fortress by Philippe Auguste in 1190, it has been added to and altered by his successors. When Louis XIV moved his court to Versailles, he abandoned the Louvre to artists, sculptors and other squatters. The Revolutionaries made it a public museum in 1793. As the home of the *Vénus de Milo* and *Mona Lisa*, the Louvre drew almost unmanageable crowds until President Mitterrand ordered its re-organisation in the 1980s. An enormous new reception area was excavated (revealing parts of the original fort), topped by the superb glass **Pyramid** designed by Sino-American architect I.M. Pei in the Cour Napoléon, which now marks the museum's main entrance.

The palace's royal chapel, **St-Germain l'Auxerrois**, dates back to 1200, but has preserved little of its Romanesque and Gothic beginnings. Its bell tolled the signal in 1572 for Catholics to start the St Bartholomew Day massacre of Protestants *(see page 16).*

Palais-Royal

The Palais-Royal, across the rue de Rivoli from the Louvre, was built as Cardinal Richelieu's residence in 1639 (it became "royal" when Anne of Austria moved in with young Louis XIV). This serene, arcaded palace, with its garden of lime trees and beeches – and the pond where Louis XIV nearly drowned – has had a past as colourful as its spectacular flower beds. In the days of Philippe d'Orléans, Prince Regent while Louis XV was a child, the Palais-Royal was the scene of notorious orgies. A later duke (another Philippe) added apartments above the arcades, along with two theatres (one now the venerable Comédie Française), shops, gambling houses and fashionable cafés. In the ferment that led

Once the epicentre of city scandal, the Palais-Royal now houses the French Ministry of Culture.

up to the Revolution, it was a scene of furious debate. On 13 July 1789 a young firebrand orator, Camille Desmoulins, stood on a table at the Palais-Royal's Café de Foy to sound a call to arms. The Bastille was stormed the next day.

Despite efforts to curry favour with the revolutionaries, such as calling himself Philippe Egalité (equality), the duke ended up on the guillotine with the rest of the family. After the Revolution, the palace became a gambling den again and narrowly escaped destruction in the 1871 uprising. Once it was restored, between 1872 and 1876, the palace became respectable. Today, it houses the Ministry of Culture, Council of State and the Constitutional Council. Some of the shops still exist, and the sumptuously decorated Grand Véfour restaurant looks just as it did 200 years ago.

In 1986, an artist installed rows of black-and-white striped stone columns in the main quadrangle, known as the **Cour d'Honneur**. Some are short, some are tall, but a few are just the right height for sitting on.

Next to the Palais-Royal stands the **Banque de France**, east of the garden (and landlord of most of its apartments), and the **Bibliothèque Nationale** (National Library), just to the north. This began as a royal library in 1368, when Charles V placed 973 manuscripts in the Louvre. Most of the millions of books, engravings and ancient manuscripts it has accumulated over the centuries have been transferred to the new national library on the Left Bank *(see page 57)*. The old building with its splendid *Salle de Travail* (reading room, 1863) is being transformed into a research library of specialist collections for scholars.

Les Halles

East of the Palais-Royal, Les Halles was for centuries the site of the capital's central food markets (now in a more spacious, if less colourful, location at Rungis, near Orly). To widespread regret, Victor Baltard's great cast-iron and glass pavilions were torn down in the 1970s. Eventually, gardens, children's playgrounds and the maze-like, partly subterranean shopping mall, **Forum des Halles**, transformed the site. Saturdays bring throngs of teenagers from the suburbs to shop, watch films, roller skate, munch fast food, and hang out. The liveliest meeting place is around the monumental Renaissance **Fontaine des Innocents** (once part of a cemetery). Bars, restaurants

The Fontaine des Innocents was once part of a cemetery, but is now a popular hangout.

and late-night brasseries line the adjoining rue Berger and the streets leading off it. Clubs and discos come alive at midnight and stay open until dawn, especially on weekends. Away from the gardens and playgrounds, the quarter has its seedy side: drink and drugs, pickpockets and prostitutes. Rue St-Denis, once primarily a red-light district, is now pedestrianised, but still has its share of sex shops.

The remarkable church of **St-Eustache** dominates the north side of Les Halles. Built from 1532 to 1637, the main structure is late Gothic with a somewhat incongruous but imposing Renaissance colonnade on its western façade. The church is renowned for its choral concerts and recitals on the grand organ designed by Baltard, architect of Les Halles.

Beaubourg

East of the Forum des Halles, streets closed to traffic and lined with cafés, brasseries, art galleries and boutiques link up with the startling **Centre Georges-Pompidou**. This avant-garde multimedia cultural centre, which also houses the Musée National d'Art Moderne *(see page 74)*, reopened in January 2000 after lengthy renovation. Controversy raged for years after the 1977 opening of this colourful "oil refinery". The comparison came as no surprise to the architects, Italy's Renzo Piano and Britain's Richard Rogers, who deliberately left the building's service systems visible – and colour-coded. Now, as with the Tour Eiffel and the Louvre's Pyramid, people have learned to live with it and even love it.

Besides its permanent art collections and popular public library, ingenious exhibits cover every aspect of contemporary life, artistic and technological, and the aesthetics of consumer culture. There is a particular emphasis on young people. The place also offers a terrific view. Pay the museum admission, then take the **lifts** running in transparent tubes from the bottom left- to the top right-hand corner and see Paris unfold before your eyes. The sloping **plaza** outside is one of Paris' most popular locations for street performers.

Place Vendôme

Louis XIV wanted this most elegant of Paris squares to provide an imposing setting for a monument to him. After it was laid out in 1699, only Louis' financiers could afford the rent. Now, the Ministry of Justice shares the square with banks, famous jewellers and the Ritz Hotel. Like all royal statues, that of Louis XIV was overthrown during the Revolution. Its replacement, the Vendôme column, commemorates in bronze relief the victories of Napoléon, cast from 1,250 Austrian

Of the inside-out design of his namesake cultural center, Georges Pompidou said, "That'll get them screaming."

cannons captured at Austerlitz and topped by a statue of the emperor. It, too, was toppled, during the 1871 Commune at the instigation of painter Gustave Courbet, who had to pay the crippling cost of having it re-erected two years later.

Opéra-Garnier and the Grands Boulevards

Make your way past the goldsmiths and furriers of the rue de la Paix to the ornate opera house (now named after its architect Charles Garnier to distinguish it from the new Opéra-Bastille; *see page 52*). Begun at the height of Napoléon III's Second Empire, it was completed only in 1875, after the Commune. It is the epitome of the exuberance of a city regarding itself as Europe's most glamorous capital, an impression that is underscored by the grand foyer and staircase. The five-tiered auditorium, with its incongruous modern ceiling painted by Chagall in 1964, holds a mere 2,000 spectators. Underneath the building is a small lake which provided the inspiration for the phantom's hiding place in Paul Leroux's *Phantom of the Opera*. Now the home of the national ballet company, the house was renovated in 1995.

A stock exchange, the Bank of France, a theatre: these were among the various uses proposed for the huge neoclassical church, **La Madeleine**. Napoléon wanted it as a temple of glory for his army, but his architect suggested the Arc de Triomphe instead. The restored monarchy opted for a church, as originally intended when building started under Louis XV. It was finally consecrated in 1842. Climb the steps for a great view down the rue Royale to the place de la Concorde and National Assembly beyond.

Musée Jacqemart-André, at 158 boulevard Haussmann, is not far from the Madeleine. Housed in the splendid mansion

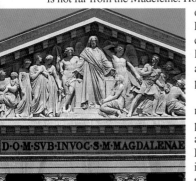

of 19th-century art collector Edouard André, the museum contains a fine collection of Italian Renaissance, Flemish and 18th-century French paintings.

The **Grands Boulevards**, running from the Madeleine past the Opéra-Garnier and all the way to place de la Bastille, comprised the fashionable heart of Paris from the 1860s until well into the 20th century. They are less

The neoclassical edifice of La Madeleine offers a great view down the rue Royale.

chic now, but their majestic sweep can still evoke former glories. On boulevard des Capucines, retrace the footsteps of Renoir, Manet and Pissarro as they took their paintings to Nadar's house, signposted at No. 35, for the historic 1874 exhibition of Impressionism. Nowadays, popular cinemas have found an appropriate home on the boulevards, for it was at the Hôtel Scribe, near the Opéra, that the Lumière brothers staged the first public moving picture show in 1895.

Montmartre

Montmartre is really a hill-top village (*"La Butte"* to its residents), with narrow, winding streets and dead-ends. For the past 200 years it has been associated with artists and bohemians. The *Montmartrobus* spares you the walk and shows you some of the area in a single tour, but the best way to discover Montmartre at your own pace is to start early, at the top. Take the métro to Abbesses and the lift to the street (the stairs here are endless) and notice the handsome Art Nouveau entrance as you leave. Rue Yvonne le Tac leads to the base station of a funicular railway. It was here that St Denis is said to have been martyred *(see page 13)* and where St Ignatius Loyola launched the Jesuit movement in 1534.

The funicular (it takes métro and bus tickets) climbs to the terrace in front of the Byzantine-style basilica of **Sacré-Cœur**. Standing at the highest point in Paris, it's one of the city's principal landmarks, and one of the few to remain perennially controversial. Artists still scorn it as a vulgar pastiche, and the working-class residents of the area resented it being erected as a symbol of penitence for the insurrection of the 1871 Commune – they didn't feel in the least penitent. The Sacré-Cœur's conspicuous whiteness comes from the local Château-Landon limestone, which bleaches on contact with carbon dioxide in the air and hardens with age. For many, the best reason for visiting the basilica is the view of the city from the dome or the terrace below.

Just a few steps west of Sacré-Cœur is **St-Pierre-de-Montmartre**, one of the city's oldest churches. Consecrated in 1147, 16 years before the church of St-Germain-des-Prés *(see page 58)*, it is a significant work of early Gothic style, belied by its 18th-century facade. The Sacré-Cœur's architect, Paul Abadie, wanted to demolish St-Pierre, but he was overruled, and it was restored "as a riposte to the Sacré-Cœur".

Nearby **place du Tertre** was once the centre of village life. Try to visit during the early morning, before the mass-production artists set up their easels and the crowds of tourists take over.

In place Emile Goudeau, just downhill but artistically on an altogether much higher level, No. 13 was the site of the studio known as the **Bateau-Lavoir** (so-called because the building resembled the Seine's laundry boats, before it was destroyed by fire). It was here, if in any one place, that modern art was born: Picasso, Braque and Juan Gris developed Cubism; Modigliani painted in a style all his own; and Apollinaire wrote his first Surrealistic verses. Some of their predecessors – Renoir, van Gogh and Gauguin – once lived and worked just north of place du Tertre in rue Cortot, rue de l'Abreuvoir, and rue St-Rustique.

On rue St-Vincent at the corner of rue des Saules, look out for the city's last surviving **vineyard**, the tiny Clos de Montmartre, producing a wine that reputedly "makes you jump like a goat."

At the far end of rue Lepic, a market street renowned for its food shops, is place Blanche, where everything suddenly changes. You hit boulevard Clichy, or it hits you. Right on the corner is the Moulin Rouge, still staging its nightly cabarets, mostly to package tourists. All the way east to **place Pigalle** and beyond runs a ribbon of tawdry nightlife, with sex shops, peep shows and other dubious attractions, punctuated by a few conventional restaurants and bars.

The principal **cemetery** of Montmartre, where luminaries of the arts such as the composers Berlioz and Offenbach lie buried, may seem a world away, but it's only a short walk west from the Moulin Rouge to the entrance (west past the Moulin Rouge, then right at avenue Rachel).

The Byzantine-style basilica of Sacré-Coeur – an ongoing subject of artistic controversy.

Le Marais

The district to the north of Ile de la Cité and Ile Saint-Louis has bravely withstood the onslaught of modern construction. It provides a remarkably authentic record of the development of the city, from the reign of Henri IV at the end of the 16th century to the advent of the Revolution. Built on reclaimed marshland, as its name suggests, the Marais contains some of Europe's most elegant Renaissance mansions *(hôtels)*, many of which now serve as museums and libraries. The biggest change is the recent influx of trendy boutiques and gay bars.

Take the métro to Rambuteau and start at the corner of the rue des Archives and the rue des Francs-Bourgeois, named after the poor (not bourgeois at all) allowed to live here tax-free in the 14th century. The national archives are stored in

moment among the many tall tombs
others veritable miniature chapels.
available at the entrance) guide
...

aise, northeast of the Bastille, has
urials since its foundation in 1804.
in 1871, when the Communards
s Fédérés in the southeast corner
were executed by firing squad.
those of painter Ingres, dancer
posers Rossini and Chopin, who
s such as La Fontaine, Molière,
de – honoured with a fine monu-
buried here. More recent arrivals
Signoret and singer Jim Morrison,

The tranquil **Cimetière de Montmartre**, below the hill, has
an equally illustrious roll-call: Berlioz (buried with Harriet Smith-
son, who inspired his *Symphonie Fantastique*), Offenbach, Degas,
Feydeau, Nijinsky, the great chef Carême, the filmmaker François
Truffaut and Louise Weber, credited with inventing the cancan.

In the **Montparnasse** cemetery are the tombs of composers
Saint-Saëns and César Franck, writer Maupassant and poet Baude-
laire, plus Alfred Dreyfus, the Jewish army officer whose conviction
on trumped-up spying charges split the nation. Also buried here
are car maker André Citroën, Vichy prime minister Pierre Laval
(executed while dying from a suicide attempt) and philosopher
Jean-Paul Sartre and his writer companion Simone de Beauvoir.

Beneath Montparnasse, the subterranean **Catacombs** are old
quarries whose corridors were used in the past for the reburial
of millions of skeletons removed from overcrowded cemeteries and
charnel houses. Unidentified, they are stacked on shelves, piled
in heaps, or artfully arranged into macabre patterns. It can be
cold and damp, but if skulls and bones appeal, find the main entrance on place Denfert-Rochereau. Shortened to Denfert, it sounds
just like the old name, *Place d'Enfer*, or Hell Square.

an 18th-century mansion, **Hôtel de Soubise**. Across a vast, horseshoe-shaped courtyard, you come across the exquisite rococo style of Louis XV's time in the apartments of the Prince and Princess of Soubise. Up on the first floor is the **Musée de l'Histoire de France**, with gems such as the only known portrait of Joan of Arc painted in her lifetime and the diary kept by Louis XVI. His entry for 14 July 1789, the day the Bastille was stormed, reads *Rien* (Nothing).

A garden (not always open to the public) connects the Hôtel de Soubise with its twin, **Hôtel de Rohan**, on the rue Vieille du Temple. In particular, look out for Robert le Lorrain's fine *Les Chevaux d'Apollon* over the old stables in the second court-yard, widely considered to be one of France's most beautiful 18th-century sculptures.

Also on the rue des Francs-Bourgeois, Hôtel Carnavalet, once home of the lady of letters, Madame de Sévigné, is today the **Musée Carnavalet** dedicated to the history of Paris *(see page 75)*. The **Musée Picasso**, nearby at 5 rue Thorigny, is housed in the beautifully restored Hôtel Salé *(see page 71)*.

The rue des Francs-Bourgeois ends at what most agree is the loveliest residential square in Paris, **place des Vosges**. Henri IV had it laid out in 1605 on the site of an old horse-market, his idea (borrowed from Catherine de' Medici) being to have "all the houses in the same symmetry." After the wedding festivities of his son Louis XIII, the gardens became the fashionable place to promenade, and later a spot for aristocratic duels. Today, there's a children's playground and it is perfect for just sitting around.

One of the best times to see the square's architecture is in the winter time, when the chestnut trees are bare and don't obscure the worn pink brick and honey-coloured stone facades. Victor Hugo, author of *Les Misérables*, lived at

No. 6, which is now a museum housing many of his manuscripts, artefacts and collection of drawings.

While in the Marais, take a wander through the old **Jewish quarter**. Jews have lived around the **rue des Rosiers** for centuries. More recent arrivals from the Jewish communities of North Africa have largely replaced the Ashkenazim of Eastern Europe, who themselves took the place of the Sephardim who first settled in Paris from Spain in the 13th century. This lively area has delicatessens, kosher butchers and even kosher pizza shops.

Bastille

The large, circular **place de la Bastille** is enjoying a new lease on life. No trace remains of the prison stormed in 1789; even the column in the centre commemorates a later revolution, that of 1830. For many years a run-down area, it was given a shot in the arm by the construction of the **Opéra-Bastille**, one of President Mitterrand's *Grands Projets*. This opened in 1990 to a chorus of hostile comment. Critics attacked Carlos Ott's building as an unimaginative misfit. At least the acoustics were rated a success, and the new home of the National Opera is now an accepted part of the rich cultural life of Paris.

In the adjacent streets, such as rue de la Couronne, traditional shops alternate with art galleries, artists' studios and restaurants. To the northeast of the Opéra, in rue de la Main d'Or, rue de Lappe and their offshoots, clubs and discos have revived an old nightlife tradition.

LEFT BANK

The fashion and media worlds are gradually supplanting the intellectuals in their time-honoured stronghold on the Left Bank *(rive gauche)*. Writers and painters who used to congregate in the cafés of St-Germain-des-Prés frequently find themselves squeezed out by film directors, TV personalities, advertising people and more and more tourists. There is much more to the Left Bank than the student life of the Latin Quarter, but so many schools and colleges are packed into a small area that it's the young who set the pace.

Montparnasse took over from Montmartre as the haunt of the avant-garde in the 1920s and the area still stakes a claim. The Left Bank has its share of monuments and museums, and Les Jardins du Luxembourg remain an evergreen favourite.

Latin Quarter

As far back as the 13th century, when Paris's first university moved from the cloisters of Notre-Dame to the Left Bank, the young came to the *quartier* to learn Latin. Here, the tradition of scholastic enquiry has often evolved into a spirit of protest and outright revolt before subsiding into a lifelong scepticism.

In ancient days the university simply meant a collection of scholars who met on a street corner or in a public square or courtyard to listen to a lecture given from a bench or balcony.

Now the tradition of openair discussion continues over coffee or a glass of wine on

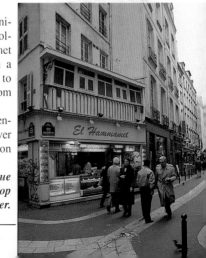

Stop by a Greek barbecue or Tunisian pastry shop along the Latin Quarter.

some café terrace or another on the boulevard St-Michel or in the streets around the faculty buildings.

The quarter also includes France's two most prestigious high schools, the Lycées Henri IV and Louis le Grand, training grounds for France's future elite.

Begin your visit to the Latin Quarter at the **place St-Michel**, where students buy their books and stationery or gather around the grandiose 1860s fountain by Davioud. From here, plunge into the narrow streets of the **St-Séverin** quarter to the east (rue St-Séverin, rue de la Harpe and rue Galande). You will discover medieval streets full of smoky Greek grills, Tunisian bakeries selling sticky date and almond pastries, and art-house cinemas.

Little **St-Julien-le-Pauvre**, a jewel of early Gothic architecture dating from between 1165 and 1220, hosts recitals of chamber and religious music. With its wafting incense and Masses said in Greek or Arabic (the church belongs to the Melchite sect of the Greek Orthodox Church), St-Julien is not out of place in an area packed with Middle Eastern restaurants. Just across rue St-Jacques stands the exquisite 13th–15th-century Flamboyant Gothic **church of St-Séverin**, in which Dante is said to have prayed and Saint-Saëns asked to be made honorary organist.

> Truly Parisian friends exchange kisses once on each cheek – twice or more is often considered "provincial" or "suburban."

The Sorbonne

Named after the 13th-century college established by Robert de Sorbon for poor theological students, the university was later taken in hand by Cardinal Richelieu, who financed its reconstruction (1624–1642). Few of the somewhat forbidding buildings are open to the public, but you can go inside the 17th-century **courtyard** with its ornate sundial and see the outside of the baroque library and domed church. Protest against over-crowding, antiquated teaching, bureaucracy and the very basis of the social system made the Sorbonne a focal point for unrest in 1968, a year of ferment throughout Europe. Over on the quiet, tree-shaded **place de la Sorbonne**, it's hard to imagine the police invading such a peaceful sanctuary – one that for centuries guaranteed student immunity. But invade they did, and revolt exploded onto the streets. Students and workers made common cause, and there followed widespread national strikes that threatened the survival of the government. In the aftermath of the revolts, the Sorbonne was absorbed into the huge Paris Universities monolith and lost its independence.

Standing virtually opposite the Sorbonne's rue des Ecoles entrance, at 6 place Paul-Painlevé, are the massive brick ruins of the ancient Roman public baths. They survived as part of an abbey – now the **Musée National du Moyen Age**, still often called by its former name, Musée de Cluny (see page 72). Its most famous exhibits are the wonderful 15th-century **tapestries**, including the Lady with the Unicorn.

Panthéon

A stroll up the rue St-Jacques past the highly reputed Lycée Louis le Grand leads to the gigantic neoclassical **Panthéon**. Designed for Louis XV as the church of Ste-Geneviève (1755), it was secularised during the Revolution to serve as a mausoleum. For most of the 19th century the Panthéon oscillated between secular and consecrated status, according to the current régime's political persuasion. Finally Victor Hugo's gigantic funeral in 1885 settled the issue in favour of a secular mausoleum. Novelist Emile Zola, socialist leader Jean Jaurès, Léon Gambetta (leader during the 1870 siege of Paris), Louis Braille (inventor of the blind alphabet), Pierre and Marie Curie

The Panthéon provides a noble backdrop to this statue in the Luxembourg Quarter.

(discoverers of radium, honoured only in 1995; Marie being the Panthéon's first woman), and many other national heroes are interred here.

The bare interior is bleak, its windows covered up by the monumental 19th-century murals painted by Puvis de Chavannes. The crypt is a grim maze of corridors lined with cells containing the tombs of the famous, as well as the not-so-famous. A good display on the history of the Panthéon is the best part of the visit.

The old streets behind the Panthéon, where the bustling **rue Mouffetard** and its offshoots meet are a village within the city. The stalls of the morning market *(see page 86)* are piled with appetising produce. Here and in the tiny place de la Contrescarpe you will find a large choice of ethnic restaurants, especially Thai, Vietnamese and Chinese.

A block to the east, signs to **Arènes de Lutèce** lead you to a little park, site of a Roman amphitheatre, restored after its remains were found during the 19th century.

Jardins du Luxembourg

Bright with flowers and statues of historical figures peeping out from among the bushes, the Jardins du Luxembourg are the prettiest green space on the Left Bank. Students find quiet corners to read, relax or play tennis, and children sail their boats on the octagonal pond or ride a merry-go-round designed by none other than Charles Garnier, architect of the Opéra *(see page 45)*. Old men meet under the chestnut trees to play chess or a game of *boules*. At the north end of the gardens, the Palais du Luxembourg, built for Marie de' Medici early in the 17th century, now houses the French Senate.

East along the Seine

Back down by the Seine, but heading east, stroll past the Jussieu University complex that stands on the site of the Halles aux Vins (wine market). The **Institut du Monde Arabe** (Arab World Institute), at 23 quai St-Bernard, was built with the help of 16 Arab nations to foster cultural links between Europe and the Islamic world. The fine museum inside traces the cultures of the Arab world, both the pre-Islamic and Islamic periods, with first-rate temporary exhibits. The best way to see them is to start on the seventh floor and work down. A library of over 40,000 volumes covers all aspects of Arab culture. The view from the rooftop cafeteria is better than the food for anyone hoping to sample the pleasures of Arab cuisine, however.

The **Jardin des Plantes** next door, created by Louis XIII as "a royal garden of medicinal plants", is still an excellent botanical and decorative garden, with exotic plants in the hothouses.

The adjoining **Museum National d'Histoire Naturelle** has done a fine job of renovating its venerable exhibits of fossils, skeletons, butterflies and mineral samples. Outstanding is the superbly designed new **Grande Galerie de l'Evolution** (entrance at 36 rue Geoffroy-St-Hilaire) devoted to the origins of all life on earth.

With its four glass towers in the shape of open books, the new national library, **Bibliothèque François Mitterrand**, is the flagship building of the redeveloped Tolbiac district east of the Gare d'Austerlitz. The vast riverfront complex surrounding a sunken garden of some 250 exotic trees is popularly known as the TGB (*Très Grand Bibliothèque*: "Very Big Library"). More formally, it also bears the name of François Mitterrand, for whom it was the ultimate (but posthumous) achievement of his ambitious building programme for Paris. Opened in late 1996, it houses over 12,000,000 books and has a state-of-the-art electronic retrieval system that's open to the general public and research scholars.

St-Germain-des-Prés

This Left Bank area is one of the town's most attractive neighbourhoods. Not part of the Latin Quarter, but an extension of it, this is the home of numerous publishing houses, the Académie Française, expensive interior design and fashion shops, bookshops and café terraces ideal for people-watching.

It used to be the headquarters of Jean-Paul Sartre and his existentialist acolytes. In place St-Germain-des-Prés, the Café Bonaparte on the north side and the Deux Magots on the west provide ringside seats for a street theatre of mimes, musicians, and neighbourhood eccentrics. The Café de Flore round the cor-

The Bibliothèque François Mitterand houses some of France's oldest and most treasured works.

ner has hung on to its intellectual tradition more than the others, perhaps because of its rather ideologically confused history. It's been a home-away-from-home for the extreme right Action Française group under Charles Maurras in 1899; the poet and surrealist precursor Apollinaire in 1914 (who, with his friends, liked to provoke brawls); and, during the 1950s, Sartre's existentialists.

Also on the place St-Germain stands the **church of St-Germain-des-Prés**, the oldest church in Paris. It is a mixture of Romanesque and Gothic, with a clock tower dating from about the year 1000 and a 17th-century porch sheltering 12th-century doorposts. Restored after being used in the Revolution as a gunpowder factory, the church is a popular venue for concerts.

North of the square, rue Bonaparte leads past the **Ecole Nationale Supérieure des Beaux-Arts** (Fine Arts School). This structure incorporates fragments of medieval and Renaissance architecture and sculpture that make it a living museum. During the events of May 1968, students used it as a factory for militant posters.

The august Palais de l'Institut de France, home of the **Académie Française**, is on the quai de Conti by the Pont des Arts. Designed by Louis le Vau in 1668 to harmonise with the Louvre across the river, the Institut began as a school for the sons of provincial gentry, financed by a legacy of Cardinal Mazarin. Then, in 1805, the building was turned over to the Institut, which comprises the Académie Française, supreme arbiter of the French language founded by Cardinal Richelieu in 1635, and the Académies des Belles-Lettres, Sciences, Beaux-Arts, and Sciences Morales et Politiques. Guides to the Institut like to point out the east pavilion, site of the old 14th-century Tour de Nesle. They say that Queen Jeanne de Bourgogne used the tower to watch out for likely young lovers,

The boulevard du Montparnasse was once a popular haunt for artists.

whom she summoned for the night and then had thrown into the Seine.

Montparnasse

Named after the mountain home, the classical Muses, Paris's "Mount Parnassus" was a mound left after quarrying – long gone, but remaining an inspiration to artists. In the 1920s, the quarter took over from Montmartre as the stamping ground of the city's artistic colony, led by Picasso. American expatriates such as Ernest Hemingway, Gertrude Stein, F. Scott Fitzgerald and John dos Passos liked the free-living atmosphere and added to the mystique themselves *(see opposite page).*

The attraction isn't immediately evident: the wide, straight **boulevard du Montparnasse** is plain by Paris standards. Nowadays, the majority of the haunts where the "Lost Generation" found itself have been polished and painted, or even entirely rebuilt, but people still pay elevated prices for the privilege of sitting in a seat that might once have been warmed by Modigliani, Lenin or Sartre.

The 59-storey, black **Tour Montparnasse** may be an egregious eyesore, but the view from the top is marvellous (33 avenue du Maine, open daily 9.30am–10pm).

Cafés with a Past

Many of the cafés once frequented by great artists and thinkers still flourish – although today's prices have risen to match their renown.

St-Germain-des-Prés. Camus, Sartre and Simone de Beauvoir used to meet at *Les Deux Magots* at 170 blvd St-Germain, 75006. Now it attracts more tourists than philosophers (closed August). Another favourite was *Café de Flore*, right next door (closed July). *Le Procope*, 13 rue de l'Ancienne Comédie, 75006, was the first coffee-house in Paris, dating from 1686; the decor is as interesting as its legends: Voltaire reputedly drank 40 cups a day here, and the young Napoléon had to leave his hat as security.

Montparnasse. One of Henry Miller's hang-outs, *Le Sélect* (99 blvd du Montparnasse, 75006) opened as an all-night bar in 1925; les Six, the group of composers including Erik Satie and Francis Poulenc, met here. *La Coupole* opposite (102 blvd du Montparnasse, 75014) was a favourite with Sartre and de Beauvoir in the years after World War II; it has been rebuilt and now seats 400. *Le Dôme* at No.108 has lost some of its character since the days of Modigliani and Stravinsky, with elaborate remodelling. Across the street, Picasso, Derain and Vlaminck used to meet at the *Rotonde* (105 blvd du Montparnasse, 75006). At the junction of boulevard du Montparnasse and boulevard St-Michel, *La Closerie des Lilas* is where Lenin and Trotsky dreamed of a Russian Revolution, and where Hemingway and his friends met after World War I.

Right Bank. The resplendent *Café de la Paix* in Le Grand Hôtel at 12 blvd des Capucins, 75009 was a favourite with the Prince of Wales (later Edward VII) and Oscar Wilde, Zola and Maupassant. Caruso also used to dine here after singing at the Opéra across the street. Near Les Halles, *La Promenade de Vénus* at 44 rue du Louvre, 75001, was the 1920s headquarters of André Breton and his fellow surrealists. Market workers and celebrities used to share the 24-hour *Au Pied de Cochon* (At the Pig's Foot), 6 rue Coquillière, 75001. In the Marais, Lenin and Trotsky (again) met at *La Tartine*, 24 rue de Rivoli, 75004, a dark little local bar at the unfashionable end of this long street.

East of the station, the **cemetery** (*see page 50*, entrance on boulevard Edgar Quinet), is the resting-place of some famous and controversial figures in French history.

Invalides

Geographically if not temperamentally part of the Left Bank, the Palais-Bourbon is the seat of the **Assemblée Nationale** (parliament). Designed for a daughter of Louis XIV in 1722, it makes a stately riverside façade for the 7th *arrondissement*, with its 18th-century embassies, ministries and private mansions (*hôtels particuliers*). Napoléon added the Grecian columns facing the Pont de la Concorde, but the palace is more graceful seen from its entrance on the south side. Access is available only on written request or invitation by a deputy. A privileged few get to see the great Délacroix paintings in the library, illustrating the history of civilisation.

The Prime Minister's splendid residence, Hôtel Matignon at 57 rue de Varenne, is a short walk from the National Assembly. Its private park has a music pavilion favoured for secret strategy sessions. On the same elegant 18th-century street, the **Musée Rodin** at No. 77 houses the sculptor's works in the delightful Hôtel Biron (*see page 75*).

The most important sight in the neighbourhood is the monumental **Hôtel des Invalides**, established by Louis XIV as the first national hospital and retirement home for soldiers wounded in action. At one time it housed approximately 6,000 veterans, but Napoléon commandeered a large part of it for the **Musée de l'Armée** (Army Museum). Eventually, the Invalides came to symbolise the glory of Napoléon himself, when his remains were finally brought back from St Helena in 1840 for burial in the chapel under the golden **Dôme**. His son, who died in Vienna, is buried in the crypt, his remains transferred here by Adolf Hitler in 1940.

The main courtyard allows access to the adjoining church of **St-Louis-des-Invalides**, decorated with flags taken by French armies in battle. The courtyard itself contains the 18 cannons, including eight taken from Vienna, which Napoléon ordered to be fired on great occasions – including the birth of his son in 1811. The cannon sounded again for the 1918 Armistice and the funeral of Marshal Foch in 1929.

Southwest of the Invalides is the **Ecole Militaire**, where officers have trained since the middle of the 18th century. Their former parade ground, the vast **Champ de Mars**, is now a green park stretching all the way to the Tour Eiffel. Horse races were held here in the 1780s, and also five World Fairs between 1867 and 1937. In the 20th century, it became the front lawn of the Left Bank's most luxurious residences. It's also popular with American expatriates, who can frequently be seen playing touch football or softball games.

The lavish dome of Les Invalides symbolises the glory of Napoléon.

Tour Eiffel (Eiffel Tower)

What remains for most people the ultimate monument was a resounding success right from the start. In 1889, two million visitors paid 5 francs (76 cents) a head to climb to the top and it has bewitched the world ever since.

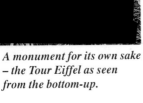

A monument for its own sake – the Tour Eiffel as seen from the bottom-up.

Some monuments celebrate heroes, commemorate victories, or honour kings or saints. This is a monument for its own sake. Its construction for the 1889 World's Fair was an astounding engineering achievement – some 15,000 pieces of metal joined by 2,500,000 rivets, soaring 320 metres (984 ft) into the sky on a base only 130 metres (430 ft) across.

At the time, it was the tallest structure in the world. Later, when radio and television were introduced, it provided the perfect perch for transmitters.

On the tower's inauguration, the lifts were not yet in operation and Prime Minister Tirard, aged 62, stopped at the first platform, 57 metres (187 ft) up, letting his younger Minister of Commerce continue to the top to present Gustave Eiffel with the Legion of Honour medal. Conceived as a temporary structure just for the Fair, the tower was slated for destruction in 1910, but nobody had the heart to take it down and it became the city's chief landmark. New illumination was installed in 1985 to light up the tower from within, and it was an obvious focus for the city's millennium celebrations.

An audio-visual show about the tower is screened on the first platform; there are restaurants on the first and second, and a bar on the third. On clear days, the view from the top extends about 65 km (40 miles), but more often the second platform offers the best view. Try to get there an hour before sunset for the best light.

WESTERN OUTSKIRTS

Bois de Boulogne

The capital's biggest park runs along the west side of the chic 16th *arrondissement*. It covers 900 hectares (2,200 acres) of grassland, lakes and woods. Napoléon III had Baron Haussmann transform this remnant of an old hunting forest along the lines of a London park. The **Bagatelle**, once a royal retreat, has a lovely English garden, bursting with flowers during spring and early summer. The **Jardin d'Acclimatation** is an amusement park with plenty of attractions for children: shows, rides and a small zoo. There are bikes for rent outside its entrance for exploring the rest of the park. The **Musée des Arts et Traditions Populaires** has excellent displays of folk art and crafts through the ages. Also within the park are a boating lake and two fine racecourses, Longchamp for flat races and Auteuil for steeplechases. But beware: in spite of police patrols, after nightfall parts of the Bois de Boulogne are reckoned to be among the most dangerous places in Paris.

La Défense

Follow the long avenue de la Grande-Armée down from l'Etoile and the battery of towers looms larger and larger beyond the elegant, leafy suburb of Neuilly. Cross the river and you are in a mini-Manhattan that has sprouted since 1969 to become a city in its own right. In the process, it has somehow managed to get a soul, in spite of the inhuman scale of some of its windswept spaces.

The **Grande Arche** is further away than most of the towers, and only when you get close do you realise just how big it is. A hollow cube 110 metres (360 ft) high and 106 metres (347 ft) wide, it could straddle the Champs-Elysées and tuck Notre-Dame underneath it. Built with remarkable speed (Danish architect Johann-Otto von Sprekelsen won the contest in 1983 and it was completed in time for the bicentennial of the French Revolution in 1989), the Grande Arche stands on an axis with the Arc de Triomphe and the Cour Carrée of the Louvre. Its white gables are clothed in Carrara marble, the outer façades with a combination of grey marble and glass; the inside walls are covered with aluminium. The two "legs" contain offices, while the roof houses conference rooms and exhibition space. Bubble lifts whisk you up through a fibreglass and Teflon "cloud", held by steel cables, but the ride to the top is expensive and the view not much more striking than from the terrace.

Increasing numbers of visitors and office-workers have given rise to more and more shops, cinemas, hotels and restaurants. One of the cinemas, near the Grande Arche, has a big wrap-around IMAX screen, and in the same building the **Musée de l'Automobile** displays over 100 classic cars, restored to mint condition. Across the main

The Grande Arche de la Défense could straddle Notre-Dame.

concourse a 12-m (39-ft) bronze thumb by César sticks out like, well, a sore thumb. Stroll down the tiers of terraces and you will find many more statues, fountains and murals by Miró, Calder and other modern artists, all detailed on street-plans given out at information desks.

MAJOR MUSEUMS

Musée du Louvre

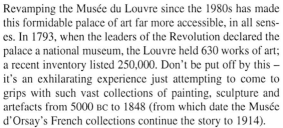

Revamping the Musée du Louvre since the 1980s has made this formidable palace of art far more accessible, in all senses. In 1793, when the leaders of the Revolution declared the palace a national museum, the Louvre held 630 works of art; a recent inventory listed 250,000. Don't be put off by this – it's an exhilarating experience just attempting to come to grips with such vast collections of painting, sculpture and artefacts from 5000 BC to 1848 (from which date the Musée d'Orsay's French collections continue the story to 1914).

The magnificent glass Pyramid designed by American architect I.M. Pei has gained acceptance as a harmonious entrance to this most venerable of French museums. An escalator descends to the reception area, which comprises shops, cafés and the ticket office. At the information counter, collect a copy of the free **handbook** with colour-coded floor plans. (Admission, too, is free on the first Sunday of every month.)

Broad corridors lead to the various parts of the museum. The museum authorities have made heroic efforts to help you find your way through the labyrinth. Each of the three main wings is named after one of France's great figures: the Richelieu wing, the Sully wing in the east, and the Denon wing beside the Seine. Each wing is then divided into numbered areas, which are shown on the floor plans (in colour). The locations of some of the most famous exhibits are pinpointed. You *will* get lost at times, but in so doing you may discover marvels you weren't even looking for.

On a first visit, you may like to spend a half-day just seeing the highlights – with time off for postcard shopping and a café break. For the collections, the *acoustiguide* (recorded tour available in English) can be useful. Some of the highlights:

Medieval Moat: The foundations and drawbridge support of a 12th-century fortress, uncovered while excavating the new entrance halls.

Egyptian: A lion-headed *Sekhmet* (1400 BC) and huge *Amenophis IV* (1370 BC).

Mesopotamian: Babylon's Mari palace paintings (2000 BC) and stone tablets of Hammurabi Code (1750 BC).

Greek: The winged *Victory of Samothrace* and beautifully proportioned *Vénus de Milo*.

Italian: Splendid sculpture of the *Two Slaves* by Michelangelo; Leonardo da Vinci's fabled *Mona Lisa*, but also his sublime *Virgin of the Rocks*; Titian's voluptuous *Woman at her Toilet*; Caravaggio's *Death of the Virgin*; the poignant *Old Man and His Grandson* by Ghirlandaio.

French: Poussin's *Arcadian Shepherds*; Watteau's melancholy *Gilles* and graceful *Embarkation for Cythera*; Fragonard's erotic *Le Verrou (The Bolt)*; Delacroix's *Liberty Guiding the People*.

Dutch and Flemish: Rembrandt's cheerful *Self-Portrait with a Toque*, his beloved *Hendrickje Stoffels*, also portrayed nude in *Bathsheba Bathing*; Van Dyke's dignified *Charles I of England*; Rubens' tender *Helena Fourment*.

Spanish: Uncompromising Velázquez portrait of *Queen Marianna of Austria*; El Greco's *Christ on the Cross*; Ribera's gruesomely good-humoured *The Club Foot (Le Pied-Bot)*.

German: Gripping *Self-Portrait* by Dürer; Holbein's *Erasmus*.

English: *Conversation in a Park* by Gainsborough.

The Louvre's illuminated glass pyramids, designed by I.M. Pei, provide a striking entrance to the museum.

Musée d'Orsay

"The station is superb and truly looks like a Fine Arts Museum, and since the Fine Arts Museum resembles a station, I suggest… we make the change while we still can," said painter Edouard Detaille in 1900. In 1986, his joke became a reality. Linked to the Right Bank Jardins des Tuileries by the new Passerelle Solférino footbridge, the converted 19th-century hotel-cum-railway station was transformed into the Musée d'Orsay, devoted to French art from 1848–1914. Keeping the exterior much as it was, Italian architect Gae Aulenti adapted the interior to house many of the previously scattered works of that period, including the superb Impressionist collections formerly held in the Jeu de Paume. Sculpture is well represented, and photography is present from its inception (1839).

Orsay is one of the easiest of great museums to navigate: the free floor plan and signs are both crystal clear. Newcomers may prefer to start at the top with the Impressionists and Post-Impressionists: Renoir, Cézanne, Manet, Monet, Toulouse-

The Musée d'Orsay is home to one of the finest collections of French art in the world.

highly imaginative way, and frequent lectures, guided tours and concerts are scheduled. There is a café high up behind a huge clock, and on the middle level the station hotel's beautifully restored restaurant is back in use. Orsay is also one of the few Paris museums that is air-conditioned – a pleasant retreat on a hot day.

Centre Georges-Pompidou

"That'll get them screaming," said then President Georges Pompidou, as he approved the plans (chosen from 681 competing designs) for the cultural centre bearing his name, but more popularly known as simply Beaubourg, after its 13th-century neighbourhood. It was re-opened in January 2000 after extensive renovation. The combination of public library (1st–3rd floor), children's and adult workshops (ground floor), *cinémathèque*, industrial design centre and music laboratory has made the complex a constant hive of activity.

The plaza outside is a popular rendezvous point for its free shows. The excellent **National Museum of Modern Art** on the 5th (1905–1960) and 4th (contemporary) floors provides a rewarding education in all the disparate art movements of the 20th century. The collections, regularly rotated from the 45,000 works in reserve, range from the Fauves and Cubism to Dadaism, Surrealism, Abstract Expressionism and all the break-away factions and reactions that followed them. The great innovators are all here: Matisse, Picasso, Kandinsky, Duchamps, Pollock, Rauschenberg and Francis Bacon, as well as sculptors Brancusi, Arp, Tinguely, Giacometti and Claes Oldenburg. The 5th floor also attracts crowds to its rooftop restaurant with superb city views.

> Remember: On Monday, the Louvre is open and the Musée d'Orsay is closed; on Tuesday, the Louvre is closed and the Musée d'Orsay is open.

Musée de l'Orangerie

A pavilion in the corner of the Jardins des Tuileries is home to the outstanding Walther-Guillaume Collection and Monet's renowned *Nymphéas* (Water Lilies). Masterpieces by Cézanne, Renoir, Utrillo, Rousseau, Modigliani, Picasso, De-rain and Soutine hang in the upstairs rooms. For his great *Nymphéas* murals, Monet himself chose the two ground-level oval rooms as those most likely to recapture the experience of coming across the water lily ponds at his home in Giverny *(closed for renovation until 2003, see page 75).*

Musée Picasso

Evoking superbly an artistic and personal biography of the 20th-century master, the museum displays over 200 paintings, 158 sculptures, and hundreds of drawings, engravings, ceramics and models for stage sets and costumes drawn from the artist's personal collection. The museum also includes works by fellow painters Braque, Matisse, Miró, Degas, Renoir and Rousseau collected by Picasso during his lifetime. Not the least of the attractions are the artist's letters, photo albums, bullfight tickets and holiday postcards.

Musée National du Moyen Age (Musée de Cluny)

The wonderful setting of this museum is alone worth a visit: an old abbey incorporating the massive remains of the city's 3rd-century Roman baths, the Thermes de Cluny. One of the exhibits is older still: the fragments of a monument to Jupiter (1st century AD) discovered near Notre-Dame. Twenty-one of the 28 heads of Notre-Dame's kings of Judah *(see page 33)*, some retaining traces of their original pigmentation (1220), were found in a bank vault and brought here. But the museum's most celebrated treasures are the late 15th-century

tapestries, in particular the *Lady with the Unicorn*, depicting the five senses and the temptations the lady vows to overcome.

Parc de la Villette: Cité des Sciences

If there's one thing this institution dislikes, it's being called a museum. First, the

Explore the 3rd-century remains of the Roman baths at the Musée National du Moyen Age.

Parc de la Villette offers a range of activities, and second, it puts the accent firmly on participation. But as with any good museum, you can learn a lot and enjoy yourself too. There's something for visitors of all ages, and for anyone ready to be excited by the world of science.

The main building has a lot in common with Beaubourg, although this one is four times bigger. A variety of themes are explored, such as space, health, communications, agriculture, etc. Some of the hands-on displays are fun, but French is sometimes needed to comprehend the information presented.

The stainless-steel Géode sphere, made of 6,433 reflecting triangles, houses a cinema with a 360-degree movie screen that is 36 metres (118 ft) in diameter. As you watch the film, you have the sensation that you are part of it. There's also a 60-seat space-flight simulator. The principal exhibition area, the planetarium and aquarium, and the decommissioned 1957 "hunter-killer" submarine the *Argonaute* are all covered by the entrance charge (or Museum Pass), but there are additional fees for some of the other activities, including the creative play areas for young children *(see page 75)*.

A canal passes right through the Parc de la Villette, so if you have time it's possible to come here by boat from central Paris (a three-hour trip; *see page 26*).

The nearby **Cité de la Musique**, on the other side of the canal, has a new concert hall, the ultra-modern buildings of the Conservatoire National (music academy), and an impressively large rock venue, the Zénith, as well as a museum containing 4,500 musical instruments (900 of which are on display). The park is at its liveliest during the summer, when various music festivals and the popular *Cinéma en Plein Air* (outdoor cinema) take place. You can obtain a complete schedule of upcoming events from the main tourist office on the Champs-Elysées.

Major Museums

Entry charges range from €5–8. Enquire about reduced rates for children, students and pensioners. Some museums charge less on Sunday. Entrance is free on the first Sunday of the month for the following museums: Louvre, Orsay, Centre Georges-Pompidou, Orangerie, Rodin, Picasso and Moyen Age.

The **Museum Pass** (*Carte Musées et Monuments*) gives entry to 70 museums and monuments in Paris and its region, including the Louvre and the Château de Versailles. Passes valid for one, three or five consecutive days can be bought at museums, tourist offices and métro stations. You'll save if you visit just two museums per day. Ask for the free booklet detailing all the museums you can visit with your pass.

These are some of the most important museums:

Musée du Louvre (The Louvre) is open Mon, Wed 9am–9.45pm, Thur–Sun 9am–6pm; closed Tues; free admission on the first Sunday in the month. Métro: Palais-Royal-Musée du Louvre *(see page 67)*.

Musée d'Orsay is the home of an outstanding collection of European art from 1848–1914. Open Tues–Sun 9am–6pm (summer); Tues–Sun 10am–6pm (winter); till 9.45pm Thur, closed Mon. Métro: Solférino RER Musée d'Orsay *(see page 69)*.

Centre Georges-Pompidou (Musée National d'Art Moderne) is an extraordinary building housing a collection that exhibits art of the 20th century. Open Mon, Wed–Sun 11am–9pm; closed Tues and 1 May. Métro: Rambuteau, Hôtel de Ville, Châtelet *(see page 70)*.

Musée d'Art et d'Histoire du Judaïsme is a new museum of Jewish art and history inaugurated in 1998 in a splendid 18th-century mansion at the heart of the old Marais district. Open Mon–Fri 11am–6pm, Sun 10am–6pm. Métro: Rambuteau, Hôtel de Ville.

Musée de l'Homme, in the 1937 Palais de Chaillot, has a formidable collection of fossils, prehistoric artefacts and ethnology from around the world. Open Mon–Sun 9.45am–5.15pm, closed Tues. Métro: Trocadéro.

Musée National du Moyen Age (Musée de Cluny) displays art from the first century of the Roman Empire to around 1500. The collection is housed in an old abbey, amid the massive remains of the Romans' public baths. Open Mon–Sun 9.15am–5.45pm, closed Tues. Métro: St-Michel, Cluny, Maubert-Mutualité *(see page 72)*.

Musée de l'Orangerie, a pavilion in the corner of the gardens, has Monet murals and the Walther-Guillaume Collection of Impressionist and post-Impressionist Art. Open Mon–Sun 9.45am–5.15pm, closed Tues. Métro: Concorde (closed until 2003).

Musée Rodin, housed in a fine 18th-century mansion and garden, has the definitive collection of works by the great sculptor. Open Tues–Sun 9.30am–5.45pm (5pm Oct–Mar), closed Mon. Métro: Varenne.

Musée Picasso displays the artist's collection of his own work as well as many pictures by his friends and contemporaries in a handsome old house and garden in the Marais. Open Mon, Wed–Sun 9.30am–6pm (5.30pm, winter), closed Tues. Métro: Chemin Vert, St-Paul *(see page 71)*.

Palais de la Découverte is mainly for children and has numerous hands-on exhibits about science and exploration, as well as a planetarium. Open Tues–Sat 9.30am–6pm, Sun 10am–7pm, closed Mon. Métro: Champs-Elysées-Clémenceau, Franklin-Roosevelt.

Musée Carnavalet (Musée de l'Histoire de Paris) features documents, engravings and paintings that bring Paris's history to life. In a remarkable exhibit devoted to the Revolution, a letter from Robespierre is stained with the author's blood: he was arrested and wounded while signing it. Open Tues–Sun 10am–6pm, closed Mon. Métro: St-Paul, Chemin Vert, Bastille *(see page 51)*.

Cité des Sciences et de l'Industrie (La Villette), situated in an extensive park on the northeastern outskirts of Paris, has ultra-modern exhibitions with plenty of audio-visual and interactive displays, 3D and 360-degree films, and much more besides, all of which is designed to educate and entertain. Open Tues–Sat 10am–6pm; Sun 7pm, closed Mon. Métro: Porte de la Villette *(see page 72)*.

EXCURSIONS

Chartres

If city life is wearing you down, then escape to the sprawling grounds of Fontainebleau.

Chartres Cathedral (inaugurated around 1200), towers above the old town and surrounding plain. Its medieval stained glass, including three stunning rose windows, is of unrivalled complexity. Climb to the roof for a view of the carved stone tracery and flying buttresses. The cathedral is situated 88 km (55 miles) southwest of Paris by the A11 or N10, or by train from Gare Montparnasse. There are bus tours from Paris. Open daily 7am–7.30pm (7.30am–7pm Oct–Mar). The crypt and tower may be closed at lunchtime.

Fontainebleau

The forest here – and the charming adjoining town – are as popular as the château. The latter was a royal palace for much longer than Versailles, with additions made over seven centuries, notably from François I in the 16th century. The old hunting forest, cool and shaded even in hot weather, is perfect for gentle walks, cycle rides, picnics, even rock-climbing.

Fontainebleau is situated 64 km (40 miles) southeast of Paris by the A6 or by train from Gare de Lyon and then bus to the château. Bus tours from Paris are available. Open Mon, Wed–Sun (closed Tues) May, June, Sept and Oct 9.30am–5pm, July–Aug 9.30am–6pm, Nov–Apr 9.30am–12.30pm and 2–5pm. Entrance is free on the first Sunday of the month.

Giverny

Claude Monet's glorious floral and water gardens are much more attractive than the rather artificially restored house. The painter lived at Giverny from 1883 to 1926 and painted the gardens many times, especially the water lilies.

Giverny is situated 85 km (53 miles) northwest of Paris by the A13, D181 and D5, or by train from Gare St-Lazare to Vernon with a shuttle bus from the station to Giverny. The house is open 30 Mar–1 Nov Tues–Sun 9.30am–6pm, closed Mon. The best time to go is in the early morning in spring.

Malmaison

Set in lovely grounds, the château used to be the home of Napoléon's wife, Josephine, who continued to live here after their divorce. Many of her possessions are on display in the various private and state apartments open to visitors.

Malmaison is located 6 km (4 miles) west of Paris. Métro: Grande Arche de La Défense, then bus 258, or RER to rueil-Malmaison, and then walk. Open May, June, July Mon–Fri 10am–5.45pm, Sat–Sun 10am–6pm; April, Aug, Sept Mon–Fri 10am–12.30pm and 1.30–5.45pm, Sat–Sun 10am–6pm; 1 Oct–31 Mar closes at 5.15pm.

Vaux-le-Vicomte

A 17th-century château designed by Le Vau, Le Nôtre and Le Brun for Louis XIV's finance minister, Fouquet. No sooner was the project completed than the king had its owner arrested for embezzlement and jailed for life.

Vaux-le-Vicomte is situated 56 km (35 miles) southeast of Paris on the N5 or by train from Gare de Lyon to Melun, and then taxi. Open 11 Mar–12 Nov Mon–Fri 10am–1pm and 2–6pm, Sat–Sun 10am–6pm. Candlelit visits 7 May–mid Oct, 8pm–midnight Thurs and Sat.

Versailles

Louis XIV, the "Sun King", was quite simply a megalomaniac, but he also had extraordinary vision. He was wary of Paris and its rabble (all too easily roused) and rising aristocracy (ever-demanding and arrogant). What better way to keep potential trouble-makers under his thumb than to coop them up at Versailles, and let them squabble for rights and privileges as futile as attending His Majesty's awakening?

Versailles is as extravagant, formidable, and vainglorious as the man himself. Louis XIII had hoped to turn his favourite hunting ground into a modest retirement home, but his son and heir made it the centre of a universe, proclaiming his own grandeur in an edifice of brick, marble, gilt and crystal.

A visit to the château takes most or all of a day, entails a lot of walking, and shouldn't be inflicted on young children. Bus tours leave from the Jardin des Tuileries on the rue de Rivoli side but you may prefer to do things in your own time. Make an early start, travel by RER *(see page 103)*, and you can fit in a morning tour of part of the palace. Stroll through the gardens, have lunch beside the Grand Canal (a packed lunch allows you to avoid Versailles' tourist traps) and take tea in the grounds of the Petit Trianon. Finally, end your day by wandering back across the palace gardens for a last view of the château at sunset.

The central section of the building is where the royal family lived. Conceived by Louis Le Vau, Jules Hardouin-Mansart and landscape designer André Le Nôtre in 1661, it was completed 21 years later. Le Vau also designed the marble courtyard, decorated with 84 marble busts.

Highlights of the vast interior include the **Royal Chapel**, a gem of high baroque; the **State Apartments**, in which Louis XIV used to entertain; the Salon de Diane, where he would try his hand at billiards; and the glittering **Hall of**

Mirrors *(Galerie des Glaces)*, 73 metres (240 ft) long and built to catch the setting sun in 17 tall, arched panels of mirrors. Adjoining it is the King's Bedroom, where Louis died of gangrene of the leg in 1715. In the Queen's Bedroom, 19 royal children were born, the births often attended by members of the public, as was the custom. Several parts of the château, including Louis XV's superb **Royal Opera**, have to be visited on separate guided tours.

The most impressive façade faces west, to the gardens; the fountains begin to play at 3.30pm on three Sundays a month, from May to September. You should also look at the **Grand Trianon**, the small palace that Louis XIV used on occasions when he wanted to get away from the château. The **Petit Trianon**, favoured by Louis XV, and the marvellous **Hameau** (little village) and miniature farm where Marie-Antoinette,

Versailles is every bit the reflection of its creator Louis XIV
– extravagant, formidable, and vainglorious.

queen of Louis XVI, played at being a shepherdess are also worth a visit. They're some way from the château and each other; a little train runs a shuttle service.

Versailles is situated 24 km (15 miles) southwest of Paris, by road (N10); or by train from Gare St-Lazare to Versailles; or by RER (line C5) to Versailles-Rive Gauche; or by métro to Pont de Sèvres, then bus 171. The château is open Tues–Sun 9am–6.30pm (5.30pm Oct–Apr); the Grand and Petit Trianon is open daily noon–6.30pm (5.30pm Oct–Apr); the gardens are open daily dawn till dusk. Entrance free first Sunday of the month.

Disneyland Paris Resort

Much more than a theme park, Disney's ambitious recreation complex also encompasses hotels, camping facilities, restaurants, a convention centre, a championship golf course, tennis courts and several swimming pools.

In the theme park itself, Main Street USA, recapturing the traditions of small-town America at the turn of the 20th century, leads to four other "lands" – Frontierland, Adventureland, Fantasyland and Discoveryland. Each themed section has a variety of fun experiences to offer. Hosts Mickey and Minnie Mouse, Goofy, Donald Duck and Pluto wander around in their familiar costumes, posing with visitors. Every day at 3pm there's a spectacular all-singing, all-dancing parade including floats inspired by the famous Disney movies. For further information, tel: 01 60 30 60 30.

The resort is situated 32 km (20 miles) east of Paris, close by Marne-la-Vallée. A motorway *(autoroute)* gives access from the city and the airports, Charles-de-Gaulle and Orly. Speedy commuter trains (RER line A) from the capital and even faster long-distance trains (TGV) serve Marne-la-Vallée/Chessy station near the entrance.

WHAT TO DO

However delightful, sightseeing in Paris is only part of the pleasure of a visit. The shops, ranging from high-fashion salons and small speciality shops to flea markets, are among the best in the world. The town also provides plenty of opportunities for both fitness enthusiasts and fans of spectator sports. Dining out *(see page 92)* is also a serious business in Paris, and as for cultural entertainment, Paris offers a wide variety of plays, films and music.

SHOPPING

The majority of shops and department stores open 9.30 or 10.30am–7pm Tues–Sat. Some shops close for lunch from noon until 2pm and many are closed on Monday mornings, if not all day Monday. The first to open its doors is usually the bakery *(boulangerie)*, and there's always a small grocer *(épicerie)* or mini-supermarket in which you can shop until 9 or 10pm, or even midnight. The success of the Marais district's Sunday opening hours is gradually spreading across town. The pharmacy at the top of the Champs-Elysées is open 24 hours a day for snacks, take-out food, books, gifts and essentials.

Department stores. The old **Galeries Lafayette** on boulevard Haussmann stocks a wide range of clothes at all price levels; fashion shows are held at 11am on Wednesdays and also on Fridays in summer. The china department is huge, and the cosmetics, sportswear and luggage sections are excellent. **Au Printemps** next door, has the biggest selection of shoes and is famous for its perfumes, toys and innovative household goods. Fashion shows are held there at 10am on Tuesdays as well as on Fridays in summer. FNAC belongs to the newer, younger generation of department stores. Branches up at l'Etoile, down the Champs-Elysées, Montparnasse and the Forum des Halles, as well as La Défense, have huge selections of books, CDs and cassettes, electronics and sports goods. **Virgin Megastore**, on the Champs-Elysées and beneath the Louvre, has the best stock of CDs in town.

Typically French is **Le Bon Marché** at métro Sèvres-Babylone, which has an excellent men's department and a fabulous lingerie section. At **La Samaritaine** opposite Pont-Neuf (at 75 rue de Rivoli), you'll find everything from home furnishings to pets, and a splendid view of the city from its 10th-floor terrace. ʙʜᴠ, beside the Hôtel de Ville, is also very popular. For cheap bargains, check out the **Tati** chain at Barbès-Rochechourart and République, with astonishing jewellery outlets on rue de la Paix and boulevard St-Germain.

The Galeries Lafayette – your chance to view fine Parisian architecture while shopping for fine Parisian fashions.

The large modern **shopping malls** include the Forum des Halles, Centre Maine-Montparnasse and the Palais des Congrès at Porte Maillot.

Fashion and accessories. Paris still leads the fashion world. Most of the *couture* houses are concentrated on the Right Bank close by the rue du Faubourg-St-Honoré (just "le Faubourg" to regular shoppers) and classier avenue Montaigne where **Christian Lacroix**, **Chanel**, **Calvin Klein**, **Hermès**, **Christian Dior**, **Yves Saint Laurent** (now retired) and **Versace** have shops. From here and the area between Les Halles and place des Victoires, *haute couture* houses and ready-to-wear *(prêt-à-porter)* boutiques have spread to the Left Bank around St-Germain-des-Prés.

Stores such as **Dorothée-Bis**, **Benetton** and the less expensive Tati are found throughout the capital. Children's clothes are fun and stylish too, though you may balk at the prices at **Jacadi**, **Oilily** and **Tartine et Chocolat**. For good, fashionable basics visit one of the many Du Pareil au Même or Sergent Major shops.

Antiques. Antiques shops cluster around the Left Bank's 6th and 7th *arrondissements*. The Carré Rive Gauche, bounded by quai Voltaire, boulevard St-Germain, and rues du Bac and des Sts-Pères, is something of a museum of ancient Egyptian, Chinese, pre-Columbian, African and Polynesian art, as well as Louis XV, Second Empire, Art Nouveau and Art Deco. Across the river, 250 dealers are concentrated in the Louvre des Antiquaires, by the place du Palais-Royal (open Tues–Sun 11am–7pm; closed Sun July and Aug), and other antiques dealers are scattered around Les Halles.

Flea markets *(Marchés aux Puces)*. The experts leave few real bargains among the old treasures, but it's fun to keep looking. Many of the stands are run by professional dealers. The giant of the flea markets is **Clignancourt** just north of

Porte de Clignancourt métro station (open 7am–7pm Sat, Sun and Mon). In the vicinity is the **Marché au Puces de St-Ouen** (open 10am–6pm), which is loaded with antiques fit for a king and accordingly priced. The market at Porte de Vanves in the 14th *arrondissement* has a high proportion of junk but lots of hidden treasure (open Sat–Sun 7.30am–5pm). You'll find bric-a-brac and second-hand clothes at Porte de Montreuil, in the 20th *arrondissement* (open Sat, Sun and Mon am). For inexpensive new clothes, pay a visit to the **carreau du Temple**, in the 3rd *arrondissement* (open every morning except Mon).

Books. Trade in old and new books flourishes on the Left Bank in or around the Latin Quarter, notably at the Odéon. Second-hand bookshops, commonly known as *bouquinistes*, line the quays of the River Seine, especially between Pont St-Michel and Pont des Arts. It's worth rummaging through the mass of books, prints, postcards and periodicals for occasional finds, though the asking prices are high.

If you're looking for English-language books, **Village Voice** on rue Princesse in St-Germain-des-Prés is a good

---

VAT Exemption

Visitors from outside the European Union staying less than three months in France can claim exemption from sales taxes (TVA) if they spend more than €200 on one or more purchases from a single shop. EU residents do not qualify. Department stores and luxury goods shops are used to dealing with foreign visitors. Staff provide a form, *bordereau de vente* (export sales invoice), known more simply as a *détaxe*, which must be stamped by customs on departure from France or the EU and then posted back to the store to reclaim the tax. The shop eventually sends you a refund in Euros. You'll generally get reimbursed faster if you pay by credit card.

choice, but try, too, **Brentano's** at 37 avenue de l'Opéra, or **W.H. Smith** at 248 rue de Rivoli.

Food and drink. Fine foods can make great presents. Thanks to today's packaging methods, it's possible to transport a wide range of foodstuffs (but remember the bans on some food imports in many countries). Two famous luxury grocery shops, **Fauchon** and **Hédiard**, compete on place de la Madeleine. For **wines**, the **Nicolas** chain has a good range at its 150 Paris branches. A bigger selection is at **Legrand**, on rue de la Banque. Spirits (liquor) and liqueurs may, for non-EU travellers, be less expensive at the duty-free shops at airports and other points of exit, though these tend to have a comparatively small choice.

Food markets. Covered markets or street markets operate all over Paris. On the Left Bank, try the photogenic **rue de**

Bouquinistes *along the Seine – rummage through a vast selection of old books and prints.*

Buci in St-Germain-des-Prés, open every morning except Monday. Most popular with tourists is **rue Mouffetard** (open am only Tues, Thurs and Sat) behind the Panthéon. On the Right Bank, the Wednesday and Saturday market on **avenue Président-Wilson** has the special elegance of the 16th *arrondissement*.

The **flower market** on place Louis Lépine, near Notre-Dame on Ile de la Cité, opens 8am–7.30pm daily. On Sundays it switches to small pets, especially caged birds (open 8am–7pm). The flower stalls on place de la Madeleine open Tues–Sun 8.30am–7pm and close Mon.

SPORTS

Try *le jogging* – or more leisurely, *le footing* – in the big parks of the Bois de Boulogne and the Bois de Vincennes, on the Champ du Mars under the Tour Eiffel, along the quays beside the Seine and in the Jardins des Tuileries. The hilly Parc Montsouris (on the Left Bank) and the Buttes-Chaumont (on the Right Bank) are more challenging. An alternative is to hire a **bicycle** or **in-line skates** *(see page 103)*. Ask at tourist offices for information on bike tours of the city and outlying areas such as Fontainebleau.

The few public **tennis** courts in Paris are on a first-come-first-serve basis, as at the Jardin du Luxembourg. Big hotels may arrange for guests to play at one of the local tennis clubs.

Municipal pools are available for **swimming**. The most serious action takes place at the Olympic-size indoor pools in the Centre de Natation, at 34 boulevard Carnot, and the Forum des Halles shopping complex.

Among **spectator sports**, pride of place goes to **horse-racing**. The summer meetings at Longchamp (the venue of the Prix de l'Arc de Triomphe), Auteuil and Chantilly are as elegant as at Britain's Ascot. The serious punter who wants to avoid the frills and the Champagne can have a very good time at Vincennes and Enghien trotting races.

Rugby and football (soccer) can be seen at the spectacular Stade de France on the northern outskirts at St-Denis or at Parc-des-Princes at the south end of the Bois de Boulogne. Nearby, **tennis tournaments** are held at Roland-Garros, or indoors over at the Palais Omnisports de Paris-Bercy, near the Gare de Lyon. Paris-Bercy is also the venue for everything from rock concerts to tango competitions, as well as cycle races and indoor windsurfing.

ENTERTAINMENT

For comprehensive listings of what's on in Paris while you are there, buy one of the weekly guides, *Pariscope* (with an English-language supplement) or *L'Officiel des Spectacles*.

The cinema is a great national passion, with over 300 different **films** showing in Paris every week. For undubbed versions with French subtitles, look out for the letters VO (*version originale*) in listings or posters. Cinemas on the Champs-Elysées, in Montparnasse, St-Germain-des-Prés, Bastille and the Forum des Halles all show VO films.

Keeping up with the latest in **discos** and **clubs** can be a full-time job for professional night-owls: there's no point in

Street performers provide a bit of comic relief in front of the Place du Palais-Royal.

turning up before midnight. Many are nominally private, which means you only get in if the doormen like the way you look. Some of the more exclusive establishments are located around the Champs-Elysées, including Régine's in the rue de Ponthieu. Louder, less expensive and younger places come and go around Bastille and Oberkampf. There's still some life in St-Germain-des-Prés and the Latin Quarter, especially in university term time – making local friends is the best way to find it.

Pop and rock concerts are held at the spectacular Zénith in the Parc de la Villette (métro: Porte de Pantin), at Parc-des-Princes (métro: Porte de St-Cloud), and also the Palais Omnisport de Bercy (métro: Bercy). Ticket offices *(billeteries)* at FNAC or Virgin Megastore, both on the Champs-Elysées, will show what groups are in town.

The French take their **jazz** seriously, and Paris has many jazz clubs. Hot Brass (La Villette) and The New Morning (rue des Petites-Ecuries) attract big American and European musicians, while Le Dunois (rue Dunois) is an intimate place, cultivating more avant-garde music. The Lionel Hampton club at the Méridien Etoile (Porte Maillot) has a full programme of guest performers. The old-established Caveau de la Huchette (rue de la Huchette in St-Germain-des-Prés) opens every night at 9.30pm for listening and dancing to a small combo or a big band swing or bebop the night away. Entrance prices of around €10–20 may include your first drink; extra drinks cost anything from €5–10.

In the realm of **classical music**, Paris has come back into its own, with many fine concerts staged at Salle Pleyel and Théâtre des Champs-Elysées. There is also opera at the new Opéra-Bastille and ballet at the Opéra-Garnier. In all cases, some seats are fairly reasonably priced, though these tend to be sold out rapidly. Look out for free concerts in churches.

Modern **dance** is enjoying a revival, with a new wave of

Innocent fun can be found around just about every corner – here, goofing around at the Palais-Royal courtyard.

small, imaginative companies beginning modestly at the Café de la Danse (passage Louis-Philippe) and Théâtre Garnier before reaching the heights of the Théâtre de la Bastille.

French-speaking **theatre** lovers can enjoy the classics by Molière, Racine or Corneille at the Comédie Française (rue de Richelieu) or avant-garde productions at the Bouffes du Nord (Porte de la Chapelle) and Cartoucherie (Bois de Vincennes).

Floor shows keep the "naughty" image of Paris alive. The Folies Bergères (rue Richer), which launched the careers of Josephine Baker, Mistinguett and Maurice Chevalier, and the Lido on the Champs-Elysées, are both classic survivors. The most modern-day show – erotic, brilliantly choreographed and bordering on chic – is at the Crazy Horse Saloon (avenue George V). Toulouse-Lautrec painted the showgirls of the Moulin Rouge (place Blanche) over a century ago, and it still offers tourists a boisterous floor show in the old tradition. The rest of Pigalle plumbs the lower depths with a certain fascinating glee.

PARIS FOR CHILDREN

A lot of the activities that interest adults will appeal to children as well. Boat trips *(see page 26)* are good fun for everyone. The **Jardin d'Acclimatation** in the Bois de Boulogne *(see page 65)* is a special children's park, with a small zoo, pony rides, puppet shows and other attractions (open daily 10am–6pm). The main zoo, **Parc Zoologique de Paris** (open 9am–5.30pm, till 6pm Apr–Sep), is located in the Bois de Vincennes (métro: Porte Dorée) on the eastern outskirts.

Small children are bound to enjoy the merry-go-round, puppet theatres (not July and August) and pony rides in the **Jardin du Luxembourg**. They can also watch the toy boats capsize in the fountain. For the scientifically minded, there's a great deal to learn in the Cité des Sciences et de l'Industrie at **La Villette** *(see page 72)*. The **Palais de la Découverte** *(see page 75)* makes use of a similar hands-on approach.

Some 30 km (20 miles) outside Paris at Marne-la-Vallée, the **Disneyland Paris Resort** could keep kids happy for several days *(see page 80)*. Fans of the Astérix comics about ancient Gaul and the Romans will enjoy the **Parc Astérix** theme park, near *Autoroute* A1 between Roissy (Charles-de-Gaulle airport) and Senlis (open mid-Apr–Oct 10am–6pm; mid-July–Aug 9.30am–7pm; tel. 03 44 62 34 34). **France Miniature** (open Apr–15 Nov 10am–7pm, till 11.30pm on Sat in Aug) is a 5-hectare (7½-acre) relief map of France including model villages, châteaux and monuments to a scale of 1:30 (RER train to St-Quentin-en-Yvelines, then bus).

Calendar of Events

January. *Prêt à Porter Paris*, spring ready-to-wear fashion shows at Paris-Expo, métro: Porte de Versailles. *Chinese New Year*, Chinatown, 13th *arrondissement*, métro: Porte d'Ivry.

Spring. *Foire de Trône* (late March–early May), monster fun-fair in Pelouse de Reuilly, Bois de Vincennes, métro: Porte Durée.

March/April. *Paris Film Festival*, Champs-Elysées, métro: Franklin-Roosevelt. *Paris Marathon* ends on the Champs-Elysées.

Good Friday. *Archbishop of Paris's Cross procession* up steps of Sacré-Coeur basilica, Montmartre, métro: Anvers.

May/June. *French Open Tennis Championships*, chic Grand Slam event, Roland Garros stadium, métro: Porte d'Auteuil.

June. *Feux de la St-Jean* (mid-June), with fireworks on the Seine. *Fête de la Musique* (21st), with free concerts all over Paris. *Course des Garçons et Serveuses de Café*: 500 waiters race through the grands boulevards and St-Germain-des-Près.

July. *Bastille Day* (13th, 14th), parade along the Champs-Elysées, fireworks at Trocadéro, dancing in the place de la Bastille. *Tour de France* ends on the Champs-Elysées; Night-time fireworks and illuminated fountains at Versailles (July–Sep).

September. *Journée du Patrimoine*, open day at otherwise off-limits government and private buildings.

October. *Prix de l'Arc de Triomphe*, France's biggest horse race, Longchamp, Bois de Boulogne, métro: Porte d'Auteuil and free shuttle-bus. *Festival d'Automne*, annual festival of theatre, music and dance. Until December.

November. *Beaujolais Nouveau* (third Tuesday of the month) celebrated in bars.

December. Notre-Dame packed for 11pm *Christmas Eve Mass*. *New Year's Eve* crowds on the Champs-Elysées, with fireworks at Trocadéro.

EATING OUT

Dining out is one of Paris's greatest pleasures. Indeed, for some visitors, it's the main objective of their visit. If you have a particular restaurant in mind it's best to reserve in advance (far ahead for the famous names). Otherwise, finding a place to eat is part of the enjoyment. In areas where restaurants are concentrated, take a look at a few, sharpening your appetite while you stroll around. Most restaurants display priced menus outside, so you can compare them and discover the day's specials *(plats du jour)*. One of the best signs of a good restaurant is a crowded interior, especially if it contains plenty of locals (though such places may be empty early in the evening). If the wait for a table is too long, make a reservation for another day *(see Recommended Restaurants, page 133)*.

Where to Look

No part of Paris is lacking in good places in which to eat out, but some areas offer an especially wide range.

One of the best ways to enjoy Paris is from a café terrace like this one on the Rue de Medicis.

On the Left Bank, try the area between boulevard St-Germain and Pont-Neuf, around rue St-Séverin, in the rue Mouffetard and its extension, rue Descartes, and in the area around boulevard Montparnasse. On the Right Bank, start by looking around Les Halles and Beauborg, place de la Bastille and the Marais – including the Jewish quarter. Further to the west, look between place de l'Opéra and boulevard Haussmann, to the north of the Champs-Elysées, and also near avenue Wagram, north of place des Ternes.

From mid-July to the end of August, many restaurant owners close up and go off on holiday, reducing the choice.

Menus

A boon to everyone on a budget is the fixed-price *table d'hôte* or *menu fixe*, *prix fixe* or just *menu* (remember, the French word for menu is *carte*). The word *formule* similarly

---

Economy Measures

- Find a tasty-sounding *formule* or *menu* and try to avoid ordering any extras.
- Remember, restaurants often cost less at lunchtime. Consider making lunch your main meal.
- Try the unfashionable parts of Paris, such as the east and northeast, where you will find many excellent ethnic restaurants.
- Buy sandwiches, in baguette bread, from bakeries and grocery stores (prices get inflated at sandwich bars near the main tourist sights). Better still, pick up ingredients for a picnic at one of the mini-supermarkets, and look for a bench in a park or beside the Seine.
- Fast-food establishments, including the usual international names, are found all over the city. A big step up in quality but still budget-priced are local chains such as Hippopotamus and Bistro Romain.

---

means an all-inclusive special deal. There's frequently the option of a starter plus a main course *or* a main course and a dessert (or cheese). A drink may be included in the price – either a small carafe of wine, a beer, soft drink or mineral water. In this case you may see the letters BC *(boisson comprise)* or VC *(vin compris)*.

Competition has done wonders in recent years and, in general, you get what you pay for, so a €12 formule will be simple and the portions probably quite small. If you are on a tight budget, watch out for high-priced extras, such as apéritifs or coffee, which can add up to as much as the basic meal. Never order anything without knowing the price.

Tax and service charge are included *(service compris)*. There is no obligation to do so, but an extra tip of up to 5 percent in cash is much appreciated. In theory, restaurants must provide a designated non-smoking area, but avoiding smokers is a difficult feat in Paris. Be polite about asking others not to smoke – the French do not consider it a crime.

Dealing with French Waiters

Legend has it that the word *bistro* originated in the cafés of the Palais-Royal. Impatient Russian Cossack officers, on leave in Paris in 1814 at the end of the Napoleonic Wars, are said to have called for service in Russian: *bystro*, "quick!" However impatient you are today, try to remember that French waiters like to be called *Monsieur*, not *Garçon*, and waitresses *Madame* or *Mademoiselle*. But whatever you call them and despite their haughty reputation, don't be in awe of them. They do not bite. If they do bark, bark back. They are not ogres by nature. They grow testy only if you seem aggressive – much like the rest of us.

The Options

At traditional, rather formal **restaurants**, with their own style and special dishes, people usually reserve a table, dress with at least casual elegance, and do not hurry the meal. There are many other possibilities (although the boundaries between them are blurred). A **bistro** is likely to be small, informal and family-run, and might have lace curtains, tiled floors, wood panelling and check tablecloths. Modern versions may go in for vivid colours, high-tech lighting and strange furniture. Wine comes by the carafe, plus a few bottles, per-

Paris is probably not the best place to go for those watching their weight.

haps listed on the back of the single-page menu. A *bistro à vin* (wine bar) makes more of its wines and less of its food, which may be bread and cheese, sausages and quiches. A **pub** in Paris can be a facsimile of a British or Irish pub, usually with a range of beers and hot meals as well. Beer comes bottled or draught *(pression)*, which costs less. A *demi* is 50cl, less than a pint.

A *brasserie* combines the functions of a bar, café and restaurant and keeps long hours: some never close at all. They are simply furnished, brightly lit and can be huge. You can order anything from a drink to a snack or full dinner. Alsatian cuisine is common.

A *café* sells more than just coffee: you can have a beer, apéritif, soft drink, snack or even a hot dish of the day *(plat du jour)*. You pay more sitting at a table than at the stand-up counter – a cup of coffee, for example could cost twice as much, but you can linger over it for hours. Coffee, incidentally, is *un express* (a small black coffee), unless you specify otherwise (*crème* or *au lait* is with hot milk).

> On French menus, *entrée* means starter. The main dish is called a *plat*.

It is the custom of some older people to meet at a **salon de thé** for a pastry or slice of fruit tart and afternoon tea. Some salons will serve a light lunch too.

Despite this broad choice, **vegetarians** tend to have much more limited options. In practice, it's easy to avoid meat, with plenty of salads, fish, cheese- and egg-based dishes, and restaurant chains, as well as some discerning chefs, are starting to list vegetarian choices.

Ethnic Variations

Parisians have taken to ethnic restaurants in a big way, and nowadays you can find almost as many variations as nations at the UN. Chinese restaurants were among the first, and many of them are now luxurious establishments around the Champs-Elysées area and Les Halles. Vietnamese, Laotian and Cambodian restaurants are an increasingly common sight, with dozens of places to be found in the Latin Quarter and the 13th *arrondissement*, behind the place d'Italie, which is home to numerous immigrants from Southeast Asia. Their cuisines feature distinctive flavours of mint, coriander, lemongrass *(citronelle)* and ginger, and contain a great variety of seafood. Thai restaurants have multiplied in Paris, as they have in almost every Western capital. More and more Japanese restaurants are also appearing each year, with the large number of Japanese tourists demanding a certain degree of authenticity.

Riches of the Regions

Every part of France proclaims the superiority of its cooking. Paris, with no distinctive cuisine of its own, is a showcase for them all.

Burgundy produces *bœuf bourguignon*, beef simmered in red wine with mushrooms, small white onions and a little bacon. The region's Bresse poultry is considered France's finest, and Charolais beef provides the most tender steaks.

Lyon is renowned for its pork, game, vegetables and fruit. Onion soup *(soupe à l'oignon)* is a local invention; *à la lyonnaise* generally means sautéed with onions.

Alsace is next to Germany, and has some similar dishes – smoked pork, dumplings and *choucroute* (sauerkraut, or pickled cabbage).

Brittany serves its shellfish on a bed of crushed ice and seaweed, as a *plateau de fruits de mer*. It will often include raw oysters, steamed mussels, clams, scallops, prawns and whelks.

Normandy is famous for its dairy farms. Cream and butter are staples, while the local apples *(reinettes)* turn up with flambéed partridge *(perdreau flambé aux reinettes)* and in *poulet au Calvados* (chicken in apple-brandy sauce). Besides Camembert cheese, sample the stronger Livarot or Pont-l'Évêque.

Bordeaux gave its name to *bordelaise* sauce, made with white or red wine, shallots and beef marrow, served variously with entrecôte steaks, ceps or lamprey eels *(lamproies)*.

Provence makes the most of its garlic, olives, tomatoes and the country's most fragrant herbs. Spicy *tapenade*, an olive and anchovy paste, is delicious on toast. *Daube de bœuf* is beef stew with tomatoes and olives, and then there's the celebrated *bouillabaisse* (fish stew).

The southwestern regions of **Gascony** and **Périgord** are famous for *foie gras* (goose liver) and *confit d'oie* and *confit de canard*, rich roast goose and duck.

In a Montparnasse café you can watch dusk settle on the city from a seat once warmed by Picasso or Hemingway.

Greek, Turkish and Lebanese restaurants are scattered along the Left Bank, notably in the Latin Quarter. The working-class suburb of Belleville in the northeast, home to a sizeable Algerian and Moroccan community, has the most authentic North African cooking.

Italian restaurants may be found virtually everywhere, but they are rarely very good. Indian food is making headway, going beyond simple curries and tandoori to include sophisticated Mughal and Kashmiri cuisines, though usually at inflated prices.

Wines

The French rarely feel the need to mention anything that isn't French on their wine lists. The great names of Bordeaux and Burgundy, and of course Champagne, still command the world's respect, but there's a host of other regional wines, too, which are much more reasonably priced.

Usually only the top-flight restaurants have wine waiters *(sommeliers)*. They will be happy if you seek their advice, and probably unruffled if you don't. Elsewhere, the regular waiter or waitress will take your wine order. Mark-ups are generally high (three to four times that of wine store prices), so unless you see a known favourite, it's just as well to go for a carafe *(pichet)* of the house wine *(vin de la maison)*. Most French people will be doing the same.

In summer, don't be surprised if the red wine comes chilled *(frais)*. It's the custom, and an easy one to get used to. And don't be afraid of ordering red wine with fish dishes. The French do.

To Help You Order...

Do you have a table?	**Avez-vous une table?**
I would like (a/an/some)...	**J'aimerais...**
The bill, please	**L'addition** (or **la note**) **s'il vous plait**

beer	**une bière**	mineral water	**de l'eau**
butter	**du beurre**		**minérale**
bread	**du pain**	sparkling/	**gazeuse/**
cheese	**du fromage**	still	**plat**
chips (fries)	**des frites**	pepper	**du poivre**
coffee	**un café**	salad	**une salade**
dessert	**un dessert**	salt	**du sel**
fish	**du poisson**	seafood	**fruits de mer**
glass	**un verre**	soup	**de la soupe**
meat	**de la viande**	sugar	**du sucre**
menu	**la carte**	tea	**du thé**
milk	**du lait**	wine	**du vin...**

... and Read the Menu

agneau	lamb	jambon	ham
asperges	asparagus	langouste	rock lobster
bar	sea bass	lapin	rabbit
boeuf	beef	moules	mussels
caille	quail	nouilles	noodles
canard	duck	oignons	onions
caneton	duckling	petits pois	peas
cerises	cherries	pintade	guinea fowl
champignons	mushrooms	poire	pear
charcuterie	cold cooked meats/sausage	poireaux	leeks
		pomme	apple
chou	cabbage	pomme de terre	potato
choufleur	cauliflower	porc	pork
crevettes roses/grises	prawns/ shrimps	poulet	chicken
		raisins	grapes
crudités	raw vegetables	ris de veau	calf's sweet breads
daurade	sea bream		
échalotes	shallots	riz	rice
épinards	spinach	rognon	kidney
farci	stuffed	rouget	red mullet
foie	liver	saucisse	sausage
fraises	strawberries	saumon	salmon
framboises	raspberries	thon	tuna
haricots verts	green beans	truite	trout
homard	lobster	veau	veal
huitres	oysters		

So how would you like your steak?

very rare	**bleu**	medium	**à point**
rare	**saignant**	well done	**bien cuit**
medium-rare	**rose**		

HANDY TRAVEL TIPS

An A–Z Summary of Practical Information

A

ACCOMMODATION (see also CAMPING, YOUTH HOSTELS and the list of RECOMMENDED HOTELS on page 124)

Paris has hotels to suit every taste and budget. The city is a popular destination all year round, so booking in advance in any season is recommended. During big commercial fairs, rooms are hard to find.

Hotels are officially classified into five categories, from one to five stars, determined by comfort and amenities; a complete booklet is available from the Paris tourist information office. Rates naturally depend on the hotel's amenities and location, and are posted visibly at reception desks.

Relatively few hotels have air-conditioning, but it rarely gets so hot that you'd miss it. Still, you might want to have the windows open in summer, so ask for a room that doesn't face a noisy street.

For a long stay you might consider renting. Travel sections of national newspapers carry advertisements; the *International Herald Tribune* and FUSAC (France-USA Contacts), available at expatriate hangouts and embassies, list accommodations for rent.

Do you have a single/ double room for tonight?	**Avez-vous une chambre pour une/ deux personnes pour cette nuit?**
What's the rate per night?	**Quel est le prix pour une nuit?**

AIRPORTS *(aéroport)*

Paris has two main airports. Roissy-Charles-de-Gaulle is about 30 km (19 miles) northeast of the city and has two terminals: CDG1 for most international flights; CDG 2 mainly for Air France flights. Orly (for most domestic and several international flights) is 18 km (11 miles) to the south, also with two terminals, Orly-Sud and Orly-Ouest. Both airports have exchange facilities, good restaurants, snack bars, post offices, duty-free shops and shuttle buses between terminals.

Regular AIR FRANCE **buses** (tel: 08 92 35 08 20) link the two main airports with Paris and each other, and run every 15 minutes from 5.45am–11pm. The city terminals *(aérogare)* for Charles-de-Gaulle airport are at Porte Maillot, near l'Etoile, and at Opéra (rue Scribe); you can also board the bus at the Arc de Triomphe (avenue Carnot).

Roissybus from Opéra takes about 45 minutes. Orly is also served by AIR FRANCE buses from the Invalides and Gare Montparnasse *aérogares* (40-minute journey) and by the *Orlybus* (every 15 minutes to/from Denfert-Rochereau RER station, a 30-minute journey).

Taxis are plentiful, but more expensive from the airport *(see page 120)*.

Privately run **shuttle buses** operate between city and airports, and are cheaper than taxis, but more expensive than public transport. Rates vary depending on the number of passengers: Paris Airport Shuttle, tel: 01 42 21 46 74 <www.paris-airport-shuttle.com>; Paris Shuttle, tel: 01 43 90 91 91 <www.parisshuttle.com>.

RER **trains** run every 15 minutes from 5.30am–11.30pm between Charles-de-Gaulle airport and Gare du Nord, Châtelet-Les Halles and the Left Bank; the trip takes 35–45 minutes. Orly is served by *Orlyval* trains which connect with RER line B (opposite platform) to central Paris; alternatively, use RER Line C which runs to the Gare d'Austerlitz, St-Michel and Musée d'Orsay stations: journey time is 35 minutes.

Hotel reservations can be made in airport arrival halls. At CDG 1 go to Porte 36, where a desk opens from 7.30am–11pm. (A deposit of 12 percent is required, which will be deducted from the bill.) Alternatively, the electronic noticeboard next to the desk enables you to contact (free of charge) a wide range of hotels throughout the city. CDG 2 has similar amenities. For further general information, call 01 48 62 22 80 (Charles-de-Gaulle) or 01 49 75 15 15 (Orly). Most staff speak English.

B

BICYCLE HIRE (RENTAL) *(location de bicyclettes)*
You can rent bikes by the day or week from Paris-Vélo, 2 rue du Fer à Moulin, 75005; tel: 01 43 37 59 22 <www.paris-velo-rent-a-bike.com>. **In-line skates** as well as bicycles are available from Bike & Roller, 6 rue St-Julien-le-Pauvre, 75005; tel: 01 44 07 35 89.

Many of these companies also run guided tours by bicycle; tourist information offices can supply a comprehensive list. In the Bois de Boulogne, old-fashioned bikes can be rented by the hour near the Jardin d'Acclimatation *(see page 65)*. You'll be asked for an identity document or a large deposit.

Paris

BUDGETING for YOUR TRIP

The following prices in euros should give you an idea of costs during a visit to Paris. However, they must be regarded as approximate; inflation in France, as elsewhere, pushes prices up.

Airport transfer. Bus to Orly €7.50, to Charles-de-Gaulle €10 (reduced fair for round-trips, children and groups). Train (second-class) to Orly €5.15, to Charles-de-Gaulle €7.60. Taxi to Orly €30, to Charles-de-Gaulle €40.

Bicycle rental. €14 per day, plus €200–300 refundable deposit.

Car rental (international company). Renault Clio: €90 per day, €270 per week with unlimited mileage. Renault Safrane: €150 per day, €500 per week with unlimited mileage. Tax and insurance included.

Entertainment. *Discothèque* (admission and first drink) €10–25; nightclub with dinner and floor show €60–120; cinema €6–8.

Guides. €120 for a half-day.

Hotels (double room with bath). *****(deluxe) €335; **** €230–335; ***€150–250; **€75–150; *€30–75.

Meals and drinks. Continental breakfast in hotel €6–20; in café €5–10. Lunch €15–30, dinner €30–55 and upwards, fast-food meal €4–7, coffee €1.2–2, soft drink €1–3, beer €2–7, small carafe of wine €3–5, bottle of wine €15 and up, cocktail €7–15.

Métro (tickets also valid on buses). €1.30; 10 tickets *(carnet)* €9.30; weekly ticket (city and near suburbs, Mon–Sun) €13.25; monthly €44.35, "Paris Visite" ticket €8.35 for one day, €13.70 for two days, €18.25 for three days, €26.65 for five days. Reduced rates available for children.

Sightseeing. Boats: adults €7–10, children €3–5. Monuments and museums: €5–8 (children less, or free). Museum Pass: €13 for one day, €26 for three, €39 for five days.

Taxis. The meter starts at €2.30 (with an extra 75 cents charged at train stations), and charges 55 cents per kilometre. You'll be charged 90 cents for every piece of baggage put in the boot (trunk). Night rates are higher.

C

CAMPING

The only site reasonably close to the centre of Paris is in the Bois de Boulogne, beside the Seine. It gets crowded in summer. A number of other sites are in striking distance. Try Champigny-sur-Marne, Torcy and St-Quentin-en-Yvelines, all on the RER suburban train network.

CAR HIRE (RENTAL) *(location de voitures)*

Local firms may offer lower prices than international companies, but the latter are more likely to let you return the car elsewhere in the country at no extra cost. The cheapest deals are through your travel agency before leaving home.

Among the international car hire firms operating in Paris are Avis, tel: 08 02 05 05 05 <www.avis.com>; Europcar, tel: 08 25 35 83 58 <www.europcar.com>; Hertz, tel: 01 39 38 38 38 <www.hertz.com>; Auto Europe <www.autoeurope.com>.

You must present your driver's licence (held for at least a year) and passport. You also need a major credit card, or a large deposit will be required. Minimum age for renting cars is 20–23. Third-party insurance is compulsory; full cover is recommended. The Yellow Pages *(Pages Jaunes)* lists companies under *Location d'automobiles*.

I'd like to rent a car	**Je voudrais louer une voiture**
now/tomorrow	**tout de suite/demain**
for one day/a week	**pour une journée/une semaine**

CLIMATE

Paris enjoys a mild continental climate. Extremes of heat or cold are rare, although in July and August daytime temperatures sometimes exceed 30°C (86°F). In most respects, the best seasons for a visit are spring and autumn, though winter is perfectly bearable.

The chart below is for average monthly temperatures (daily high).

	J	F	M	A	M	J	J	A	S	O	N	D
°C	8	7	10	16	17	23	25	26	21	17	12	8
°F	46	45	50	61	63	73	77	79	70	63	54	46

CLOTHING

Paris is a lot less formal than it used to be, but is still dressier than London or New York. Smarter restaurants may expect men to wear a jacket, but rarely insist on a tie. In the heat of midsummer, you will want to have light cotton clothing that you can wash and hang up to dry overnight. A raincoat is useful in winter, and an umbrella at any time. A pair of sturdy walking shoes is essential.

COMPLAINTS

If you have a complaint, make it on the spot, pleasantly and calmly, and to the correct person. At a hotel or restaurant, ask to speak to the manager (*directeur* or *maître d'hôtel*). In extreme cases only, a police station (*commissariat de police*) may help or, failing that, outside Paris, try the regional administration offices (the *préfecture* or *sous-préfecture*). Ask for the *service du tourisme*.

CRIME and SAFETY

Keep items of value and any large amounts of money in your hotel safe. Beware of being crowded by street children whose aim is to get their fingers into your pockets or handbags. Never leave a car unlocked. Don't leave anything in view when parked, and if possible remove the radio.

Any loss or theft should be reported as soon as possible to the nearest police station and to your embassy. A report will help with the insurance claim.

CUSTOMS and ENTRY REQUIREMENTS

Nationals of EU countries and Switzerland need only a valid passport or identity document to enter France. Nationals from Canada, New Zealand and the US require passports, while Australian and South African nationals must obtain a visa. For the latest information on entry requirements, contact the French embassy in your country.

As France belongs to the European Union (EU), free exchange of non-duty-free goods for personal use is permitted between France and the UK and Ireland. However, duty-free items are still subject to restrictions: again, check before you go.

For residents of non-EU countries, restrictions when going home are as follows:

Currency restrictions. There's no limit on the amount of local or foreign currencies or travellers' cheques that can be brought into France, but amounts in bank notes exceeding €7,500 (or equivalent) should be declared if you intend to export them.

D

DRIVING

To enter France by car, you will need a valid driving licence, car registration papers and insurance coverage (the green insurance card is no longer obligatory but comprehensive coverage is advisable). A red warning triangle and a set of spare bulbs are strongly recommended.

The minimum driving age is 18. All passengers are required by law to wear seatbelts. Children under 10 may not travel in the front seat (unless the car has no back seat). Driving on a foreign provisional licence is not permitted.

Road conditions. Driving in Paris can be strenuous. Despite Haussmann's broad avenues and the riverfront *voie express*, daytime traffic no longer sweeps through the capital at a tolerable speed. The ring road *(périphérique)* around Paris, in particular, gets clogged at rush hours and summer weekends. Note that tolls on motorways *(autoroutes)* outside Paris are expensive. For advance information on traffic conditions consult the 24-hour autoroute line service (with English-speaking staff); tel: 01 48 99 33 33 <www.autoroutes.fr>.

Rules and regulations. As elsewhere on the continent, drive on the right, overtake (pass) on the left. At many roundabouts (traffic circles), vehicles already on the roundabout have right of way. If this is not indicated by signs saying *vous n'avaz pas la priorité* at the approach to the roundabout then priority will be for those coming from the right. Otherwise, in built-up areas, give priority to vehicles coming from the right. In other areas, the driver on the more important of the two roads (indicated by a yellow diamond) has right of way. The use of car horns in built-up areas is allowed only as a warning. At night, lights should be used for this purpose. Don't drink and drive: random breath tests are frequent and the alcohol limit is very low (corresponding to one small drink).

Paris

Speed limits. The limit is 50 km/h (31 mph) in built-up areas and 80 km/h (50 mph) on the *périphérique* ring road. Elsewhere it is 90 km/h (55 mph), 110 km/h (70 mph) on dual highways and 130 km/h (80 mph) on *autoroutes* (toll motorways). Note: when roads are wet, limits are reduced by 10 km/h (6 mph); on motorways, the limits are reduced by 20 km/h (12 mph). In fog, the limit is 50 km/h (31 mph). Police speed traps are common, and you can be fined heavily, on the spot, for offences.

Fuel costs. Fuel *(essence)* is available as super (98 octane), normal (90 octane), lead-free *(sans plomb* – 98 or 95 octane) and diesel (gasoil). Note that many filling stations close on Sundays. Fuel on motorways is expensive: try to get to a supermarket to fill up – there can be as much as a 15 percent difference in price.

Parking. Parking *(stationnement)* is a nightmare. It is much better to walk, use the métro or take a bus. In the city centre, most street parking is metered and the spaces marked *Payant*. You buy a ticket at a nearby machine and display it inside the car. Many machines in Paris now only take a parking debit card, which can be purchased at the local *tabac*. Never park in bus lanes, express lanes or anywhere that isn't clearly permitted, or your car may be towed away.

If you need help. It's wise to take out international breakdown insurance before leaving home. Always ask for an estimate before authorising repairs, and expect to pay TVA (value-added tax) on top of the cost. Two companies that offer 24-hour breakdown service are Automobile Club Secours, tel: 08 00 05 05 24 (toll-free) and SOS Dépannage, tel: 01 47 07 99 99.

Road signs. Most signs are the standard pictographs used throughout Europe, but you may encounter these written signs as well:

Déviation	Diversion (detour)
Péage	Toll
Priorité à droite	Yield to traffic from right
Vous n'avez pas la priorité	Give way
Ralentir	Slow down

Serrez à droite/à gauche	Keep right/left
Sens unique	One way
Rappel	Restriction continues (a reminder)
driver's licence	**permis de conduire**
car registration papers	**carte grise**
Fill the tank, please.	**Le plein, s'il vous plaît.**
My car has broken down.	**Ma voiture est en panne.**
There's been an accident.	**Il y a eu un accident.**

Fluid measures

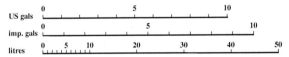

Distance

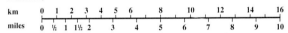

E

ELECTRICITY
You'll need an adapter for most British and US plugs: French sockets have round holes. Supplies are 220 volt, and US equipment will need a transformer. Shaver outlets are generally dual voltage.

EMBASSIES and CONSULATES
Contact your consulate or embassy only in an emergency, such as losing a passport or all of your money, a serious accident or trouble with the police. An Embassy representative can contact friends or relatives back home who can forward funds and, if necessary, put you in touch with an English-speaking lawyer.

Paris

Australia	4 rue Jean-Rey, 75015 Paris, tel: 01 40 59 33 00, fax: 01 40 59 35 38
Canada	35 avenue Montaigne, 75008 Paris, tel: 01 44 43 29 00, fax: 01 44 43 29 99
Republic of Ireland	4 rue Rude, 75016 Paris, tel: 01 44 17 67 00, fax: 01 44 17 67 50
New Zealand	7-ter rue Léonard-de-Vinci, 75116 Paris, tel: 01 45 00 24 11, fax (consulate): 01 45 01 26 39
South Africa	59 quai d'Orsay, 75443 Paris Cedex 07, tel: 01 53 59 23 23, fax: 01 47 53 99 70
UK	35 rue du Faubourg-St-Honoré, 75008 Paris, tel: 01 44 51 31 00 *Consulate*: 18-bis rue d'Anjou, 75008 Paris, tel: 01 44 51 31 02; fax: 01 44 51 31 27
US	2 avenue Gabriel, 75008 Paris, tel: 01 43 12 22 22 *Consulate*: 2 rue St Florentin, 75001 Paris (same tel as above), fax: 01 42 66 05 33

EMERGENCIES (*urgence*)

Police (*police secours*)	**17**
Fire brigade (*pompiers*)	**18**
Ambulance (SAMU)	**15**

Paris has an efficient anti-poison centre, tel: 01 40 05 48 48. You can get advice for other urgent medical problems by calling SOS Médecins at 01 47 07 77 77, SOS Help (an English-language helpline) at 01 47 23 80 80 or the SAMU at 01 45 67 50 50. For dental emergencies call SOS Dentaire at 01 43 37 51 00.

Police!	**Police!**
Fire!	**Au feu!**
Help!	**Au secours!**

G

GAY and LESBIAN TRAVELLERS

The city has a large, visible, and quite relaxed gay community: The mid-summer Gay Pride festival is a major event. Popular bars, clubs and discos are concentrated around Les Halles, Marais, and Bastille.

GETTING THERE *(see also* Airports*)*

By Air

Paris is served by two international airports: Roissy-Charles-de-Gaulle and Orly. The average journey time between Paris and Johannesburg is 13 hours, London 1 hour, New York 7 hours (less than 4 hours by Concorde), Toronto 9 hours.

Charter Flights and Package Tours

From the **UK** and **Ireland**. Most tour operators charter seats on scheduled flights at a reduced price as part of a package deal which could include a weekend or a couple of weeks' stay, a simple bed-and-breakfast arrangement, or a combined "wine tour" and visit to Paris. Among the inclusive holiday packages are tours for visitors with a common interest, such as cookery courses, school trips or art.

However, most visitors from the UK travel to France individually, either by booking directly with a ferry operator and taking a car across, or signing up for inclusive holidays which offer fly-drive and touring or self-catering arrangements.

From **North America**. ABC (Advance Booking Charters) provides air passage only (from New York, Chicago, Los Angeles and San Francisco to Paris), but OTC (One Stop Inclusive Tour Charter) package deals include airport transfers, hotel, sightseeing and meals.

Paris is the starting point for many tours of France. Wine tasting, gourmet and cooking tours, and tours of the château country are included in package deals leaving from over a dozen major US and Canadian cities, usually on a seasonal basis (Apr–Oct) and for periods of one to three weeks. You can also choose fly-drive and fly-rail options.

From **Australia** and **New Zealand**. Certain airlines offer package deals. You can also travel by independent arrangement (the usual direct direct econ-omy flight with unrestricted stopovers) or go on a fly-drive arrangement.

Paris

From **South Africa**. Excursion fares and numerous package deals are available, including Paris among other European sights.

By Car

Cross-channel operators offer plenty of special deals at competitive prices; a good travel agent will help you to find the suitable ferry for your destination. Dover–Calais is the shortest route and most convenient port from which to reach Paris.

Le Shuttle, the car transportation service through the Channel Tunnel, takes 35 minutes. The terminals are near Folkestone and Calais.

By Bus

Regular services also operate from London to Paris via cross-Channel ferries or the Channel Tunnel. Numerous lines link Paris with regional cities including Bordeaux, Lyon and Nice.

By Rail

All the main lines converge on Paris. On the ultra-rapid Eurostar TGV trains, which reach 300 km/h (187 mph), reservations are compulsory. Auto-train services *(Trains Autos Couchettes)* are also available from major towns.

The journey between London (Waterloo) and Paris (Gare du Nord) takes 3 hours by Eurostar through the Channel Tunnel. For those who arrive by ferry at the French channel ports, frequent trains run to Paris.

Tickets. Visitors from abroad can buy a *France-Vacances Spécial* pass, valid for specified periods of unlimited travel in first- or second-class, with reductions on the Paris transport network and one or two days' free car rental (with first class only), depending on the type of card.

Residents of Europe can buy an *Inter-Rail* or *Inter-Rail Plus* card, which allows one month's unlimited second-class travel on most European rail networks. The under-26 Inter-Rail card is also available for selected zones of Europe (France, Belgium, Luxembourg and the Netherlands constitute one zone). The Freedom Pass is available for travel on 3, 5 or 10 days within any month, in one or more of the 26 participating countries of Europe.

People resident outside Europe and North Africa can buy a *Eurailpass* for unlimited rail travel in 17 European countries, including France. This pass must be obtained before leaving home. Anyone under 26 qualifies for the lower-priced *Eurail Youth Pass*.

GUIDES and TOURS

Find multilingual guides and interpreters through the Office de Tourisme de Paris. Their monthly booklet *Paris Sélection* lists telephone contacts.

H

HEALTH and MEDICAL CARE (see also EMERGENCIES)

Make sure your health insurance policy covers any illness or accident while you're on holiday.

Visitors from EU countries with national health services are entitled to medical and hospital treatment under the French social security system. Before leaving home, you will need to fill in a form E111 from any post office.

Paris has excellent doctors, surgeons and medical facilities. Most large hotels and consulates have a list of English-speaking doctors and dentists. Doctors who belong to the French social security system *(médecins conventionnés)* charge the minimum.

Two private hospitals serve the Anglo-American community: the American Hospital of Paris, 63 bd. Victor-Hugo, 92202 Neuilly; tel: 01 46 41 25 25, and the Hôpital Franco-Britannique, 3 rue Barbès, 92300 Levallois-Perret; tel: 01 46 39 22 22.

Pharmacies are easily identified by the green cross they display. They are helpful in dealing with minor ailments and can recommend a nurse *(infirmière)* if you need injections or special care. One neighbourhood pharmacy is always on night-duty *(service de garde)*. Its name and address is displayed in the window of other area pharmacies. The Pharmacie Dhery, 84 ave. des Champs-Elysées; tel: (01) 45 62 02 41, is open 24 hours a day (métro: George V).

HOLIDAYS *(jours fériés)*

Public offices, banks and most shops close on public holidays, though you'll find the odd corner shop open. If one of these days falls on a Tuesday or Thursday, many French people take the Monday or Friday off as well for a long weekend (though this doesn't usually curtail activity in shops or businesses).

Paris

1 January	*Jour de l'An*	New Year's Day
1 May	*Fête du Travail*	Labour Day
8 May	*Fête de la Victoire*	Victory Day (1945)
14 July	*Fête nationale*	Bastille Day
15 August	*Assomption*	Assumption
1 November	*Toussaint*	All Saints' Day
11 November	*Armistice*	Armistice Day (1918)
25 December	*Noël*	Christmas Day

Moveable dates:

Lundi de Pâques	Easter Monday
Ascension	Ascension
Lundi de Pentecôte	Whit Monday

Are you open tomorrow?	**Est-ce que vous ouvrez demain?**

LANGUAGE

Even if your French isn't perfect, don't feel inhibited: it's better to make an effort. You cannot assume people speak English, though the younger generation increasingly does.

The *Berlitz French Phrase Book and Dictionary* covers almost all the situations you're likely to encounter in your travels; it's also available as part of the *Berlitz French Cassette Pack*. In addition, the *Berlitz French-English/English-French Pocket Dictionary* contains a glossary of 12,500 terms, plus a menu-reader supplement.

MAPS

Free city street maps are supplied by tourist information offices. Large-scale *arrondissement* (district) maps are frequently displayed at major squares and intersections, while bus shelters often have good detailed maps of the immediate neighbourhood. Most métro stations supply decent maps of the métro system, bus network and RER train system.

For longer stays, buy an indexed pocket-sized street-atlas, with a double page for each *arrondissement*, available at most tobacconists.

MEDIA

Radio and TV. You'll find Paris FM radio stations specialising in classical music, rock, and pop (French, American and, to a lesser degree, British). BBC World Service can be heard on medium-wave (648 on dial), BBC Radio 4 on long-wave (198), and Voice of America on short-wave (varying throughout the day).

Besides regular French TV channels, most hotels have a range of cable services: CNN, Sky, BBC and programmes from Germany, Japan, even Saudi Arabia, as well as French subscription channels (some carrying late-night pornography).

Newspapers and magazines *(journal; revue/magazine)*. A wide range of dailies, weeklies and monthlies is available in English and other languages. You'll find them in kiosks and *maisons de la presse*. *L'Officiel des Spectacles* and *Pariscope* (with an English-language supplement) are the most detailed weekly guides to what's on. The free monthly *Paris Sélection* (available from tourist information offices) lists concerts, festivals and shows.

MONEY (see also CUSTOMS AND ENTRY REQUIREMENTS and OPENING HOURS)

Currency. The Euro (abbreviated €) is divided into 100 cents (c or ct). Coins *(pièces)* come in 1, 2, 5, 10, 20 and 50 cents; 1 and 2 euros. Banknotes *(billets)* come in 5, 10, 20, 50, 100, 200 and 500 euros. For currency restrictions, see CUSTOMS AND ENTRY REQUIREMENTS.

Banks and currency exchange offices *(banque; bureau de change)*. Take your passport when you go to change money or travellers' cheques. Your hotel may also offer an exchange service, though at a less favourable rate. The same applies to foreign currency or travellers' cheques changed in shops, tourist offices or restaurants.

I want to change some pounds/dollars.	**Je voudrais changer des livres sterling/des dollars.**

Credit cards are widely accepted in hotels, restaurants, shops and petrol (gas) stations. Visa and MasterCard are the most common. You can usually use your card for cash advances from automatic teller machines (*DAB, distributeurs automatiques de billets*), but with the disadvantage of associated fees and interest rates. The best way to get cash is by using a cashcard. Tell your bank about your travel plans and make sure that your PIN number can be used abroad. If your card is rejected by the machine, you can go to a bank exchange counter to obtain cash with it. Visa cardholders can call toll-free 08 00 90 82 81 (no prefix) for assistance.

Travellers' cheques (with identification) are widely accepted.

Sales tax. A value-added tax (TVA) of nearly 19.6 percent is imposed on almost all goods and services, and is usually included in the price. In hotels and restaurants, this is on top of a service charge (both usually included in the quoted price).

Visitors from non-EU countries can have the TVA refunded on major purchases of goods for export (*see page 84 for details*).

Do you accept travellers' cheques/this credit card?	**Acceptez-vous les chèques de voyage/cette carte de crédit?**

 O

OPENING HOURS (*heures d'ouverture*) (see also HOLIDAYS)
Avoid using lunch hours for "administrative" tasks; although the long Parisian lunch is less common now, businesses and smaller shops may close for an hour or so, from noon–2.30pm.

Banks tend to open 9am–5pm on weekdays (some closing for lunch from noon–2pm) and close either on Sat or Mon. All banks close on major national holidays and most close early on the day before a public holiday.

Grocers, bakeries, tobacconists, food shops are open from 7 or 8am–7pm (or later, sometimes up to midnight) Mon–Sat. Food shops are often open on Sunday morning. Small shops usually close at lunchtime, 1–3pm.

Other shops, department stores and **boutiques** are open from 9, 9.30 or 10am–6.30 or 7pm (sometimes later in summer) Tues–Sat. Some close Mon am or all day Mon.

Museums are open 9, 10 or 11am–5, 5.30 or 6pm (variable). Some, including the Louvre, close Tues; others close Mon. Major national monuments, including the Arc de Triomphe, Panthéon and Ste-Chapelle are open daily, except on certain public holidays. *(See also Major Museums on page 74 and Paris Highlights on page 39.)*

P

POLICE (see also EMERGENCIES)

The blue-uniformed police who keep law and order and direct traffic are, as a general rule, most courteous and helpful to visitors. The CRS *(Compagnies républicaines de sécurité)* are the tough guys, seen wielding batons to deal with demonstrations. Outside Paris and other main cities, the *gendarmes*, in blue trousers and black jackets with white belts, are responsible for traffic and crime investigation.

If you need to call for police help, dial **17** (anywhere in France).

Where's the nearest police station?	**Où est le commissariat de police le plus proche?**

POST OFFICES *(bureau de poste)*

Look for the bright yellow sign of La Poste with its stylised blue bird. Offices are usually open Mon–Fri 8am–7pm, Sat 8am–noon (smaller post offices outside Paris close for lunch noon–2 or 2.30pm and close about 5 or 6pm). The city's main post office at 52 rue du Louvre is open 24 hours a day, every day. The post office at 71 avenue des Champs-Elysées is open until 10pm on weekdays, and opens Sun and public holidays (10am–noon and 2–8pm). A postcard to the US or the UK takes from 3 days to a week to arrive.

Apart from the usual postal services, you can send faxes and telegrams and, though no longer associated with the national telephone company, France-Télécom, you can buy *télécartes* (phone cards).

The easiest, fastest way to buy stamps *(timbres poste)* as well as phone cards is at a tobacconist *(tabac)*.

Post *(courrier)*. If you don't know ahead of time where you'll be staying, you can have your post (mail) addressed to you *poste restante* (general delivery) c/o Poste restante, 52 rue du Louvre, 75001 Paris (always open). You can collect it for a small fee on presentation of your passport. American Express, at 11 rue Scribe, 75009 Paris, performs the same service for card-holders.

The **Minitel** computer terminal, a French predecessor of the Internet, can be used for everything from TGV train reservations to booking a theatre ticket, joining a dating service, or looking up someone's telephone number or address (free of charge). Visitors can find one in most post offices: a phone card is needed to operate it. You may need help from a French person at first, although there's nothing very complicated about it. Instructions on screen are in French, but you may find a booklet in English at offices of France Télécom.

PUBLIC TRANSPORT

Bus *(autobus)*. Bus transport around Paris is efficient (and more pleasant than the métro) though not always fast. Stops are marked by green and blue signs or shelters, with the bus numbers posted, and you'll find bus itineraries displayed under bus shelters. You can obtain a general bus route plan from métro station ticket offices.

Most buses run from 7am–8.30pm, some until 12.30am. Service is reduced on Sundays and public holidays. A special bus for night-owls, the "Noctambus", runs along 10 main routes serving the capital, from 1.30am–5.30am every hour, with Châtelet as the hub.

Bus journeys take one ticket. You can buy a ticket as you board, but it's cheaper to buy a book of tickets *(carnet)* from any métro station or tobacconist. (Bus and métro tickets are interchangeable.) Punch your ticket in the validating machine when you get on. You can also buy special one-, three- or five-day tourist passes or the weekly ticket and *carte orange* (see METRO, below). Show these special tickets to the driver as you get on: **Don't** put them in the punching machine. The fine for being caught without a ticket is €20.

Métro. The Paris *Métropolitain* (*métro* for short) is one of the world's most efficient, convenient and fastest underground railway systems. It's also one of the least expensive, and it keeps growing to accommodate passengers' needs. Express lines (RER) get you into the centre of Paris from distant suburbs in approximately 15 minutes, with a few stops in between.

You get 10 journeys for the price of seven by investing in a *carnet* (book) of tickets, also valid for the bus network and for the RER, provided that you stay within Paris and don't go to outer suburbs. A special ticket called ***Paris Visite***, valid for one, three or five days, allows unlimited travel on bus or métro, and reductions on entrance fees to various attractions. A **day ticket**, *Formule 1*, is valid for métro, RER, buses, suburban trains and some airport buses.

For longer stays, the best buy is a ***Carte Orange*** (orange card), valid for unlimited rides inside Paris on métro and bus – weekly *(hebdomadaire)* Mon–Sun, or monthly *(mensuel)* from the first of the month. Ask for a *portefeuille* (ID wallet) to go with it and have a passport photo ready to stick to it. For prices, see BUDGETING FOR YOUR TRIP.

Whatever your ticket, remember to collect it after putting it through the machine at the métro entrance gates.

Métro stations have big, easy-to-read maps. Service starts at 5.30am and finishes around 1am (last trains leave end stations at 12.30am). The RATP (métro organisation) has an information office at 53-ter quai des Grands Augustins, 75271 Paris cedex. You can call them 24 hours a day at 08 36 68 77 14; website <www.ratp.fr>.

Train *(train)*. The SNCF (French Railways Authority) runs fast, comfortable trains on an efficient network. The high-speed service (TGV – *trains à grande vitesse*) operating on selected routes is excellent, but more expensive than the average train. Seat reservation on TGVs is obligatory: website <www.sncf.fr>.

The main stations in Paris are: Gare du Nord (for the Eurostar to London, and for Belgium and the Netherlands); Gare de l'Est (eastern France and Germany); Gare St-Lazare (Normandy and Calais); Gare d'Austerlitz (southwestern France and Spain); Gare Montparnasse (TGV to western and southwestern France); and Gare de Lyon (Provence, Switzerland and Italy). The TGV station at Charles-de-Gaulle Airport serves Disneyland Paris.

Validate your train ticket before boarding by inserting it in one of the orange machines (called a *machine à composter* or *composteur*) on the way to the platform. If it is not clipped and dated, the ticket collector is entitled to fine you on the train.

Taxi *(taxi)*. Taxis are reasonably priced, though there will be extra charges for putting luggage in the boot (trunk) and for pick-up at a station or airport. Also, taxis can refuse to carry more than three passengers. The fourth, when admitted, pays a €2 supplement.

You'll find taxis cruising around or at stands all over the city. Rates differ according to the zones covered or the time of the day (you'll be charged more between 7pm and 7am and on Sundays). An average fare between Roissy-Charles-de-Gaulle Airport and downtown Paris might be €35 by day, €45 at night. If you have any problems with a driver, you can register a complaint with the Service des Taxis, 36 rue des Morillons, 75732 Paris; tel: 01 45 31 14 80.

R

RELIGION

These days, a live-and-let-live atmosphere towards religion prevails, with only occasional arguments about educational funding.

Immigration has brought sizeable Jewish and Muslim communities to Paris, as well as many other smaller groups. The Yellow Pages *(Les Pages Jaunes)*, found in most hotel rooms and at all hotel desks, lists places of worship for every faith and denomination.

T

TELEPHONE *(téléphone)*

Long-distance and international calls can be made from any phone box, but if you need assistance, you can call from post offices or your hotel (you'll pay a supplement).

The system is simple, but Paris phone boxes take only **phone cards** *(télécartes)* or Visa. You can buy cards of 50 or 120 units (€7.50 or €14.90, respectively) at post offices or tobacconists.

To make an **international** call, dial 00 followed by the country code, area code (omitting any initial zero) and number. For international directory assistance, add 33 12 between 00 and the code of your chosen country, for example, 00 33 12 44 (enquiries for the UK). For assistance with American or Canadian numbers, dial 11 instead of 1 (i.e., 00 33 12 11).

The new phone system has increased all numbers to 10 digits. Paris area numbers begin with 01; Normandy and the northwest 02; Alsace and the northeast 03; Provence and the southeast 04; Bordeaux and the southwest 05. If you need help, call the operator: **12**. You need to dial all 10 digits, even within Paris.

TIME DIFFERENCES

France keeps to Central European Time (GMT + 1 hour). In summer, clocks are put ahead 1 hour (GMT + 2 hours), coming into force from late March to the end of October. With this in mind, the following chart gives **summer** time differences.

New York	London	**Paris**	Sydney	Auckland
6am	11am	**noon**	8pm	10pm

What time is it?   **Quelle heure est-il?**

TIPPING

A tip can go a long way in Paris. Service is included in restaurant bills. Increasingly, added tips are given as a token (5–10 percent) to show your appreciation for good service. Hotel staff expect to be tipped.

Hotel porter, per bag	75 cents
Hotel maid, per week	€1.50
Lavatory attendant	60 cents
Taxi driver	10–15 percent
Tour guide	10 percent

TOILETS (toilettes)

Public toilets come in the form of curved booths and are found all over Paris. They cost 30 cents to use and clean themselves after the user has left. Bars and cafés also have facilities. If you are not a customer, leave 30 or 40 cents in the dish provided or at the bar.

Paris

TOURIST INFORMATION *(office de tourisme)*

Before arriving in Paris you can obtain a lot of up-to-date information from the French National Tourist Office in your country <www.paris-touristoffice.com>. In Paris, you'll find the **Office de Tourisme de Paris** (Visitors Bureau) at 127 avenue des Champs-Elysées, 75008 Paris; tel: 08 36 68 31 12; fax: 01 49 52 53 00. Staff will be able to help you with information and booking accommodation; the office is open Mon–Sat 9am–8pm, Sun 11am–7pm, closed 1 May. You can change money there, and buy phone cards and the Museum Pass. Branches are located in major stations, the Tour Eiffel (May–Sep) and airport terminals.

For a selection of weekly events in English, call 01 49 52 53 56. For information on the region surrounding Paris, contact the CRT Ile de France, 91 ave. des Champs-Elysées, 75008 Paris; tel: 01 56 89 38 00; web site <www.paris-ile-de-france.com>.

French National Tourist Offices abroad:

Australia	25 Bligh Street, Level 22, Sydney, NSW 2000; tel: (2) 231 5244
Canada	1981 Avenue McGill College, Suite 490, Esso Tower, Montreal, QUEH3A 2W9; tel: (514) 288 4264
South Africa	Carlton Center, 10th Floor, P.O. Box 1081, Johannesburg 2000; tel: (11) 331 9252
UK	178 Piccadilly, London W1V 0AL; tel: (20) 7399 3500; fax: (20) 7493 6594
US	444 Madison Avenue, New York, NY 10022; tel: (212) 838-7800
	676 North Michigan Avenue, Suite 3360, Chicago, Illinois 60611; tel: (312) 751-7800
	9454 Wilshire Boulevard, Suite 715, Beverly Hills, CA 90212; tel. (310) 271-6665

W

WEIGHTS and MEASURES

The metric system – a French invention – is universally used.

Length

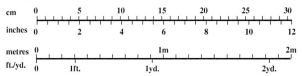

Weight

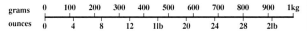

Temperature

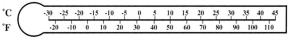

YOUTH HOSTELS *(auberges de jeunesse)*

For more information, ask for the free guide to all French Youth Hostels, obtainable from the Fédération Unie des Auberges de Jeunesse (FUAJ), 27 rue Pajol, 75018 Paris; tel: 01 44 89 87 27; <www.fuaj.org>. It is essential to reserve in advance all year round for youth hostels in Paris.

Tourist information offices offer a useful booklet entitled *Jeunes à Paris* (Youth in Paris) with addresses and telephone numbers of hostels, student halls and other low budget accommodation. (Some of these places cannot be reserved in advance.) The tourist offices may be able to arrange a reservation for you, but again, only on the same day.

UCRIF (Union des Centres de Rencontres Internationaux), <www.ucrif.asso.fr>, has three centres in Paris; BVJ, 44 rue des Bernardins, 75005 Paris, tel: 01 43 29 34 80; CIS, 43 rue de la Glacière, 75013 Paris, tel: 01 43 36 00 63; and FIAP Jean Monnet, 30 rue Cubanis, 75014 Paris, tel: 01 43 13 17 00.

Recommended Hotels

This list is divided geographically into Right Bank–Central and West (1–2, 8–9, 16–18); Right Bank–East and Ile St-Louis (3–4, 10–11, 19–20); and Left Bank (5–7, 14–15). The numbers indicate the *arrondissement* (district), also given by the last one or two figures in the postal code, e.g. 75015 is the 15th *arrondissement*.

Not all properties are wheelchair accessible. Travellers with disabilities should enquire before making reservations.

The following ranges give an idea of the price for a double room per night, with private bath, unless otherwise stated. Service and tax are included, but not breakfast. Note that prices can vary widely within a hotel, and may change according to the time of year. Always confirm the price when booking. Unless stated otherwise, all hotels accept major credit cards.

€€€€€	over 375 euros
€€€€	240–375 euros
€€€	115–240 euros
€€	65–115 euros
€	below 65 euros

RIGHT BANK–CENTRAL AND WEST (1–2, 8–9, 16–18)

Claridge Bellman €€€ *37 rue François-1er, 75008; tel: 01 47 23 54 42; fax: 01 47 23 08 84.* A small boutique hotel offering the personal touch at decent rates in the stylish district lying between the Seine and the Champs-Elysées, home of many of the great names in the fashion world. The rooms are delightfully furnished with antiques. No restaurant. 42 rooms. Major credit cards.

Costes €€€€€ *239 rue Saint Honoré, 75001; tel: 01 42 44 50 00; fax: 01 45 44 50 01.* The most sought-after hotel in Paris is just off elegant place Vendôme in this exclusive neighbourhood lined with chic boutiques. Rooms are exquisitely decorated with baroque paintings, heavy drapes and antiques. Some bathrooms have claw-foot tubs and mosaic tiles. Owner Jean-Louis Costes dislikes artificial light, so the hallways are lit with candles; even the beautiful indoor pool is dark. The celebrated café Costes is the hippest place in town. 83 rooms. Major credit cards.

Hôtel de Crillon €€€€€ *10 place de la Concorde, 75008; tel: 01 44 71 15 00; fax: 01 44 71 15 02.* This world-famous hotel forms part of the splendid classical façade dominating the north side of place de la Concorde. Renowned for its impeccable service and quality, it also has a legendary bar – favoured by foreign correspondents – and two notable restaurants, Les Ambassadeurs and the more affordable L'Obélisque. Wheelchair access. 163 rooms. Major credit cards.

Hotel Ermitage €€ *24 rue Lamarck, 75018; tel: 01 42 64 79 22; fax: 01 42 64 10 33.* This small hotel is located close to Sacré-Cœur in an old residential neighbourhood. An excellent budget choice with friendly staff and colourful bedrooms decorated in French farmhouse style. There's a lovely courtyard and terrace where breakfast is served in summer. 12 rooms. Cash only.

Hotel Keppler € *12 rue Keppler, 75016; tel: 01 47 20 65 05; fax: 01 47 23 02 29.* The best accommodation for the price in this posh neighbourhood. Rooms are large and furnished comfortably; four have balconies. There is a spiral staircase, welcoming fireplace and a bar with room service. It's all impeccably managed by the family that owns it. Forty-nine rooms. Major credit cards.

Paris

Du Louvre €€€€ *1 place Malraux, 75001; tel: 01 44 58 38 38; fax: 01 44 58 38 01*. Across from the Louvre, this recently renovated hotel has one of the most beautiful lobbies in Paris, complete with orchids and silk-covered chandeliers. The rooms are modern and spacious with Provençale touches. There's a cigar/piano bar, a library and an elegant café serving tapas-style light meals. Wheelchair access. 190 rooms. Major credit cards.

Duminy-Vendôme €€ *3–5 rue du Mont-Thabor, 75001; tel: 01 42 60 32 80; fax: 01 42 96 07 83*. Just a few steps from the pleasant Jardins des Tuileries, this is a comfortable establishment priding itself on its attractively decorated rooms: brass beds, flowery wallpaper and big marble bathrooms. 78 rooms. Major credit cards.

Four Seasons George V €€€€€ *31 avenue George V, 75008; tel: (01) 49 52 70 00; fax: (01) 49 52 70 10*. One of the most prestigious addresses in Paris, just off the Champs-Elysées, the George V re-opened in late 1999 after major renovations. Opulent as ever, the rooms are beautifully classic with modern touches and magnificent marble bathrooms. But it's the exquisite service that makes the George V one of the top hotels in the city. Wheelchair access. 245 rooms. Major credit cards.

Henri IV € *25 place Dauphine, 75001; tel: 01 43 54 44 53; no fax*. Some of the least expensive rooms in Paris can be found at this very modest budget hotel that has been popular with visiting students for decades. The good location is on charming place Dauphine across from Ile St-Louis. Rooms are somewhat old-fashioned, with shared bathrooms. Only a short walk from Notre-Dame and St-Michel. You will need to reserve well in advance. 21 rooms. No credit cards.

Lord Byron €€ *5 rue Châteaubriand, 75008; tel: 01 43 59 89 98; fax: 01 42 89 46 04.* A pleasant, small hotel, very reasonably priced for its location just east of l'Etoile, with fair-sized rooms, stylish décor and an elegant courtyard. 31 rooms. Major credit cards.

Ritz €€€€€ *15 place Vendôme, 75001; tel: 01 43 16 30 30; fax: 01 43 16 31 78.* Considered by many to be the top hotel in the world, the Ritz has welcomed the most discriminating guests for over a hundred years. Rooms are plush, decorated in Louis XV style with antique clocks and rich tapestries; many have fireplaces. The top-notch spa has a beautiful indoor pool, and there are two fine restaurants and a pleasant garden. 187 rooms. Major credit cards.

RIGHT BANK–EAST AND ILE ST-LOUIS (3–4, 10–11, 19–20)

Beaumarchais € *3 rue Oberkampf, 75011; tel: 01 53 36 86 86; fax: 01 43 38 32 86.* A pleasant budget hotel with small, modern rooms and friendly staff. Not far from the little streets and markets of the Temple quarter, and convenient to the Gare de Lyon and the Marais. 31 rooms. Major credit cards.

Des Deux-Iles €€ *59 rue St-Louis en-l'Ile, 75004; tel: 01 43 26 13 35; fax: 01 43 29 60 25.* Set in a small and attractive 17th-century mansion on the main street of the tranquil Ile St-Louis, this hotel is comfortable and friendly, with a cellar bar. Rooms are compact but attractively decorated. Reserve well in advance. 17 rooms. Major credit cards.

Jeu de Paume €€€ *54 rue St-Louis-en-l'Ile, 75004; tel: 01 43 26 14 18; fax: 01 40 46 02 76.* Delightfully situated on quiet Ile St-Louis. The hotel has kept its ancient, 17th-century *jeu de* *paume* court (a game considered the predecessor of tennis). Great for a taste of old Paris and steps to Notre-Dame. 32 rooms. Major credit cards.

Hôtel St-Merry €€ *78 rue de la Verrerie, 75004; tel: 01 42 78 14 15; fax: 01 40 29 06 82.* Arguably the most original hotel in Paris, the Saint Merry was once a 17th-century presbytery. Rooms are decorated with mahogany church pews and iron candelabra and, in one, a carved-stone flying buttress. The phone booth is in a confessional. The windows are, of course, stained glass. Affable Mr Crabbe, the owner, has devoted 35 years to renovating his Gothic masterpiece. 11 rooms. No credit cards.

Libertel Terminus Nord €€€ *12 blvd. de Denain, 75010; tel: 01 42 80 20 00; fax: 01 42 80 63 89.* This 1865 railway station hotel is right opposite the Gare du Nord in a rather bland neighbourhood. It was beautifully restored in 1993, and the rooms are attractively decorated and well equipped. The balconies of some upper-storey rooms look across to Sacré-Cœur. The 1925 Terminus restaurant is in the same building. 236 rooms. Major credit cards.

Lutèce €€ *65 rue St-Louis-en-l'Ile, 75004; tel: 01 43 26 23 52; fax: 01 43 29 60 25.* On the exclusive Ile St-Louis, this charming hotel is so small it's almost like a doll's house. Pretty, tiny rooms are attractive and very quiet. Those on the sixth floor are the most romantic. There are several excellent restaurants all around the hotel and Notre-Dame is only a two-minute walk away. 23 rooms. Major credit cards.

Pavillion de la Reine €€€€ *28 place des Vosges, 75003; tel: 01 40 29 19 19; fax: 01 40 29 19 20.* The most romantic hotel in Paris is located on the beautiful place des Vosges and feels like a country château. Rooms vary greatly in size and rate.

Most have four-poster beds, exposed wooden beams and antiques. Cosy lobby bar with evening wine-tasting; manicured gardens. 55 rooms. Major credit cards.

Rivoli Notre-Dame €€€ *19 rue du Bourg-Tibourg, 75004; tel: 01 42 78 47 39; fax: 01 40 29 07 00.* Situated on a charming narrow street in the heart of the Marais , this 17th-century building is home to a well-kept, affordable hotel. Rooms are warmly decorated with yellow or red wallpaper. Breakfast is served in a vaulted dining room with exposed stone. 31 rooms. Major credit cards.

LEFT BANK (5–7, 14–15)

Abbaye St-Germain €€€ *10 rue Cassette, 75006; tel: 01 45 44 38 11; fax: 01 45 48 07 86.* This 17th-century abbey, situated between the Jardin du Luxembourg and St-Germain-des-Prés, has been beautifully adapted into a hotel. Some rooms have original wooden beams, but all modern comforts as well. Staff are helpful and attentive. 46 rooms. Major credit cards.

Amelie € *5 rue Amelie, 75007; tel: 01 45 51 74 75; fax: 01 45 56 93 55.* A short walk from the Tour Eiffel, this friendly family-run hotel has some of the lowest rates in the area. Newly renovated rooms have small refrigerators, and all come with private baths. A narrow wooden staircase leads up to the four levels of rooms; there's no lift. Breakfast is served in the small lobby. 16 rooms. Major credit cards.

Bourgogne et Montana €€€ *3 rue de Bourgogne, 75007; tel: 01 45 51 20 22; fax: 01 45 56 11 98.* A charming hotel tucked away behind the Musée d'Orsay. The modern, spacious rooms are a bargain for this pricey neighbourhood. The large doubles are worth the extra splurge and come with double basins as well as antiques. The English-speaking staff offer concierge service to help with any sightseeing arrangements. 34 rooms. Major credit cards.

D'Angleterre €€€ *44 rue Jacob, 75006; tel: 01 42 60 34 72; fax: 01 42 60 16 93.* The location couldn't be better, on a quiet street lined with art galleries. A charming hotel that used to be the British Embassy in the 19th century; Ernest Hemingway lodged here in the 1920s. Rooms are fairly small and furnished with antiques; only the top-floor doubles are spacious. Delightful terrace and garden. 27 rooms. Major credit cards.

De L'Alma €€ *32 rue de l'Exposition, 75007; tel: 01 47 05 45 70; fax: 01 45 51 84 47.* On a very narrow and quintessentially Parisian street you'll find this small, reasonably priced hotel within walking distance of the Tour Eiffel. Students visiting the nearby American University in Paris stay here. Rooms are modern but small, the staff friendly and welcoming. 31 rooms. Major credit cards.

Hilton €€€€ *18 ave de Suffren, 75015; tel: 01 44 38 56 00; fax: 01 44 38 56 10.* One of the few large hotels on the left bank in a quiet, leafy neighbourhood steps from the Tour Eiffel. Bargains are to be had here, and frequent discounts make this luxury hotel more affordable than others. Spacious and modern rooms. Good café and well-known restaurant keep the lobby busy at all hours. Wheelchair access. 461 rooms. Major credit cards.

Hotel Familia € *11 rue des Ecoles 75005; tel: 01 43 54 55 27; fax: 01 43 29 61 77.* Location is one of the strong points of this hotel, which is within a few minutes' walk of the islands and St-Germain des Près. Familia offers solid comforts in smallish rooms for a modest price. The rooms of the fifth and sixth floor have a view of the Notre Dame cathedral. However, the main attraction for the hotel's many regular guests is the hospitable Gaucheron family who live on the premises and take pride in its every detail.

Des Grandes Ecoles €€ *75 rue du Cardinal-Lemoine, 75005; tel: 01 43 26 79 23; fax 01 43 25 28 15.* At first glance, you might think you were in the French countryside here. There are 50 large, prettily furnished rooms around a cobbled courtyard and garden of old trees and trellised roses. Although it is a short uphill walk from the métro, you are still near enough to everything, including the place de la Contrescarpe and rue Mouffetard. Major credit cards.

Lutétia €€€€ *45 blvd. Raspail, 75006; tel: 01 49 54 46 46; fax: 01 49 54 46 00.* This is one of the few large old, traditionally recommended hotels on the Left Bank. It has an Art Deco setting, and its staff are friendly and welcoming. The Brasserie Lutétia is one of the best places in Paris for fresh seafood; there's also a cigar bar and a formal restaurant. 273 rooms. Major credit cards.

Millesime €€ *15 rue Jacob, 75006; tel: 01 44 07 97 97; fax: 01 46 34 55 97.* Airy and quiet hotel on one of the most charming streets in Paris. Rooms are modern, decorated with Provençale-style bedspreads and wrought-iron lamps. Double-glazed windows and air-conditioning ensure a good night's sleep. Lovely vaulted stone breakfast room and a small garden. 22 rooms. Major credit cards.

Regent's €€ *44 rue Madame, 75006; tel: 01 45 48 02 81; fax: 01 45 44 85 73.* On a quiet street, across from the Jardin du Luxembourg. Newly renovated rooms are modern and decorated in Provençale colours. Top-floor rooms have narrow balconies with views over the Paris rooftops. Wheelchair access. 38 rooms. Major credit cards.

Relais Christine €€€€ *3 rue Christine, 75006; tel: 01 43 26 71 80; fax: 01 43 26 89 38.* Former 16th-century cloister in a quiet enclave in the heart of the bustling Odéon district, between the Latin Quarter and St-Germain-des-Prés. Rooms are a mix of modern and Louis XIII decor, with interesting touches such as wrought-iron lamps. The lush garden and courtyard are lovely on a warm afternoon. 51 rooms. Major credit cards.

Relais Medicis €€€ *23 rue Racine, 75006; tel: 01 43 26 00 60; fax: 01 40 46 83 39.* This small and attractively decorated hotel has oak-beamed rooms set around a quiet courtyard with a fountain. It is well situated, just off boulevard St-Michel and close to the Jardin du Luxembourg. 16 rooms. Major credit cards.

Rive Gauche € *25 rue des Sts-Pères, 75006; tel: 01 42 60 34 68; fax: 01 42 61 29 78.* Excellent budget choice with an unbeatable location on a calm street between St-Germain and the Seine. Rooms are sparsely and simply furnished, but all come with private baths. The exposed-stone breakfast room is charming. 21 rooms. Major credit cards.

Sainte Beuve €€€ *9 rue Ste-Beuve, 75006; tel: 01 45 48 20 07; fax: 01 45 48 67 52.* On a quiet street, steps from the excellent shops on rue d'Assas and a short walk from the Jardin du Luxembourg. Rooms are modern and warmly decorated; rooms on the top floor have skylights in the bathrooms and romantic views over the rooftops of Paris. The hotel is run by the friendly, English-speaking Monsieur Jean-Pierre Egurregy. 22 rooms. Major credit cards.

Recommended Restaurants

In this section, the term *restaurant* encompasses cafés, bistros and brasseries. Except where it is specified otherwise, the establishments listed below serve lunch from noon–2:30 or 3pm and dinner from 7 or 8pm–10:30 or 11pm. If you wish to dine particularly early or late, have your hotel's concierge call to confirm a restaurant's hours of operation. Opening and closing times can vary, particularly during August.

The price ranges quoted below are per person for a three-course dinner with a glass or two of house wine, tax and service included. Extras will send bills much higher, but conversely, a modest lunch menu can cost much less.

€€€€	over 75 euros
€€€	40–75 euros
€€	25–40 euros
€	below 25 euros

RIGHT BANK–CENTRAL AND WEST (1–2, 8–9, 16–18)

Alain Ducasse au Plaza Athénée €€€€ *25 avenue Montaigne, 75008; tel: 01 53 67 65 00.* Open for dinner Mon–Wed, lunch and dinner Thur–Fri. Cooking from France's first recipient of six Michelin stars (three apiece for two restaurants). According to Ducasse, his meals are not about fancy presentation but purity and essence of flavour. Expect truffles in abundance and superb ingredients from his native Provence. The decor is a cross between Louis XV and Philippe Starck. Major credit cards.

L'Appart €€ *9–11 rue du Colisée, 75008; tel: 01 53 75 16 34.* Open daily for lunch and dinner; Sunday brunch. Close to the

Champs-Elysées, this modern bistro looks more like someone's apartment (hence the name) with shelves of books lining the walls. The cooking is creative but not fussy: colourful salads, candied aubergine, veal with mustard seeds, fresh cod with mashed potatoes; reasonably priced wines. Major credit cards.

Le Buddha Bar €€ *8 rue Boissy d'Anglais, 75008; tel: 01 53 05 90 00.* Open weekdays for lunch and dinner; dinner only on weekends. A very trendy restaurant just off place de la Concorde, with a huge Buddha in the large, dimly lit dining room. A mix of Asian and California cuisine. Specialities include spicy crayfish with black bean aïoli and seared sesame tuna with shiitake vinaigrette. Reservations necessary. Major credit cards.

Carré des Feuillants €€€€ *14 rue de Castiglione, 75001; tel: 01 42 86 82 82.* Open weekdays only for lunch and dinner. Alain Dutournier is one of the most acclaimed chefs in Paris, so you need to reserve days ahead to dine here. His cuisine has a distinct flavour of the southwest (Armagnac). The wine list is immense. The setting is an old convent, with futuristic decor. Major credit cards.

Chiberta €€€ *3 rue Arsène-Houssaye, 75008; tel: 01 53 53 42 00.* Open weekdays for lunch and dinner, Saturday for dinner only. This elegant restaurant just beside l'Etoile has a very faithful local clientele. New chef Eric Coisel brings an innovative touch to classical *haute cuisine*. Breton lobster with Sauterne, chilled grapefruit soup with lemongrass, lamb with anise flavoured bearnaise sauce. Major credit cards.

Costes €€ *239 rue St-Honoré, 75001; tel: 01 42 44 50 00.* Open daily 7am–1am. In the fashionable hotel Costes, this café is one of the most popular in Paris. Dinner requires reservations several days ahead. Beautiful courtyard and a baroque interior with lots of crystal chandeliers. The eclectic menu includes fresh salads, Norwegian smoked salmon, and Nebraska steaks. Major credit cards.

Ladurée €€ *75 avenue des Champs-Elysées, 75008; tel: 01 40 75 08 75.* Open daily 8am–1am. Renowned in Paris for generations for its delectable macaroons, this café/bakery/restaurant is always busy and very chic. Excellent puff pastry filled with veal and mushrooms; baked cod with candied lemon. Desserts are a particular strength, especially the chestnut ice cream. Major credit cards.

Fakhr el Dine €€ *3 rue Quentin-Bauchart, 75008; tel: 01 47 23 44 42.* Open daily for lunch and dinner. Very popular formal Lebanese restaurant just off the Champs-Elysées. Small appetiser *(meze)* plates filled with tabbouleh, hummus and mouth-watering sausages; stuffed aubergine with aromatic rice in a yogurt-garlic sauce; and marinated grilled chicken kabobs are specialities. Wonderful desserts and a good selection of wines. Very attentive service. Major credit cards.

Flo € *7 cour des Petites Ecuries, 75010; tel: 01 47 70 13 59.* Open daily for lunch and dinner until 1.30am. Close to Gare du Nord. The fame of this traditional brasserie in a little back street has spread: now it runs similar establishments all around town. The original serves excellent seafood and Alsace specialities, as well as standard brasserie fare. Budget menu after 10.30pm. Major credit cards.

Guy Savoy €€€€ *18 rue Troyon, 75017; tel: 01 43 80 40 61.* Open for lunch and dinner Mon–Fri, Sat dinner only. Guy's imaginative *haute cuisine* has finally earned the highest Michelin rating, belated recognition of Paris's most inventive chef. The son of a gardener, Savoy has an obsession with vegetables that anticipated the recent trend by more than decade. He doesn't hesitate to pair truffles with lentils or artichokes. Savoy's dining room is warm and intimate and he regularly makes the rounds to greet his guests. Major credit cards.

La Maison D'Alsace €€ *39 avenue des Champs-Elysées, 75008; tel: 01 53 93 97 00.* Open 24 hours. This big, classic brasserie on the Champs-Elysées is known for Alsace specialities, especially *choucroute* (sauerkraut) and excellent seafood. The wine list includes a good selection of Alsatian wines. Pleasant outdoor seating in summer. Budget menu after 11pm. Major credit cards.

Le Grand Véfour €€€€ *17 rue de Beaujolais, 75001; tel: 01 42 96 56 27.* Open weekdays for lunch and dinner. Occupies a gorgeously ornate late-18th-century salon in the Palais-Royal, where Napoléon once took dinner with Josephine. In contrast to the traditional setting, chef Guy Martin's cuisine is modern, light and imaginative, all served on beautiful Limoges china. Among the specialities are an artichoke tart with candied vegetables and bitter-almond sorbet. Extensive wine list. Major credit cards.

Café Marly € *Palais du Louvre, 93 rue de Rivoli, 75001; tel: (01) 49 26 06 60.* Open daily 8am–2am. You can rest from your labours at the Louvre in Second Empire-style rooms facing the Pyramid or the sky-lit Cour Louvre. Very popular with models and artists, and always busy. Spinach salad with goat's cheese, tuna burger with coriander, and steak and fries are recommended. Major credit cards.

Café de la Paix € *12 blvd des Capucins, 75009; tel: 01 40 07 30 20.* The main reason to come here is the historic setting of this 1862 café; vast, gilded and mirrored, adjoining a covered terrace opposite the Opéra-Garnier. Major credit cards.

Pre Catelan €€€€ *rte. de Suresnes, 75016; tel: 01 44 14 41 14.* Open for lunch and dinner Tues–Sat, Sun lunch only. Situated in the heart of the Bois de Boulogne, this is one of the most romantic spots in Paris. Call a week ahead for reservations. *Haute cuisine* centring on fresh truffles, lobster, lamb and fresh seafood. The pastry chef is considered one of the best in France. Major credit cards.

Au Pied de Cochon €€ *6 rue Coquillière, 75001; tel: 01 40 13 77 00.* Open 24 hours. Bright and cheerful restaurant and terrace in the Les Halles quarter. Specialities are fish, big seafood platters and pigs' trotters stuffed with truffle pâté as well as budget-priced set menus. Major credit cards.

Le Safran €€ *29 rue d'Argenteuil, 75001; tel: 01 42 61 25 30.* Open daily for lunch and dinner. Close to the Opéra-Garnier. In a cheerful, intimate dining room, chef Caroll Sinclair uses only organic produce; her cuisine is steeped in Provence, and the menu changes daily. The sea bass with mushrooms and the succulent lamb simmered with thyme and red wine are specialities. Reasonably priced wines and excellent sorbets. Major credit cards.

Spoon €€ *14 rue du Marignan 75008; tel: 01 40 76 34 44.* Open weekdays for lunch and dinner. France's superchef Alain Ducasse oversees a mix-and-match culinary adventure. Choose a main course of fish or meat and then decide on sauces and accompaniments (the waiters are helpful with advice). Many of the dishes have Pacific Rim influences. Unusually for France, its wine list is full of New World vintages. Major credit cards.

Timgad €€ *21 rue Brunel, 75017; tel: 01 45 74 23 70.* Open daily for lunch and dinner. The most popular Moroccan restaurant in Paris, Timgad is warmly decorated like a mini-palace in Marrakesh. Specialities include hand-rolled couscous, lamb stews and *tagines.* Good wine list and very friendly service. Major credit cards.

Yvan €€€ *1 bis rue Jean-Mermoz, 75008; tel: 01: 43 59 18 40.* Open weekdays for lunch and dinner; Sat dinner only. Situated just off the Champs-Elysées, this elegant and intimate restaurant serves inventive cuisine prepared by the young, ever-popular chef Yvan. Specialities include pan-fried fresh fish, roasted quail with Muscat wine and beef fillet served in thin pastry with snow peas and port sauce. Excellent selection of wines. Major credit cards.

RIGHT BANK–EAST AND ILE ST-LOUIS (3–4, 10–12)

Benoît €€€€ *20 rue St-Martin, 75004; tel: 01 42 72 25 76.* Open weekdays for lunch and dinner. Traditional but expensive *cuisine bourgeoise* in a real bistro that has barely changed since it opened in 1912. Wonderful traditional French dishes such as *cassoulet,* cod with potatoes and orange ice-cream soufflé. This is a popular place, so be sure to book well in advance. Credit cards: AmEx only.

Au Châteaubriand €€ *23 rue de Chabrol, 75010; tel: 01 48 24 58 94.* Open Tues–Sat for lunch and dinner. Located close to the Gare de l'Est. The poet Jacques Prévert was a regular at Au Châteaubriand. Its decor is enhanced by fine paintings, and the rich cooking is Italian-influenced with seafood pasta and sardine lasagna the main specialities. Known for its tiramisu. Major credit cards.

Petit Bofinger € *6 rue de la Bastille, 75004; tel: 01 42 72 05 23.* Open daily for lunch and dinner. Located across from the more expensive Bofinger and close to Opéra-Bastille, this budget choice serves fine French cuisine at low prices. The bustling, lively dining room is popular with locals and visitors alike. The menu changes daily but typical dishes include salmon *carpaccio, escargots* in garlic-parsley sauce, and cod roasted with olives. Major credit cards.

La Castafiore € *51 rue St-Louis-en-L'ile, 75004; tel: 01 43 54 78 62.* Open daily for lunch and dinner. Located on the romantic Ile St-Louis, this tiny restaurant serves delicious, light, fresh Italian-French cuisine at very reasonable prices. Among the specialities are pan-fried veal with mushroom and Marsala wine sauce, tuna fillet in a spicy tomato and black olive sauce, and good hand-made ravioli. Reasonably priced wine list. Major credit cards.

Chez Casimir € *6 rue de Belzunce, 10th; tel: 01 48 78 28 80.* Open Mon–Fri lunch and dinner, Sat dinner only, closed Sun. Forget about the uninspiring decor and the unfashionable location of Chez Casimir, as it's all about serious eating here, with a menu that pays homage to fine-quality seasonal produce. Winter, for example, is strong on game and *pot au feu* – beef cooked in a fine broth with vegetables and fresh coriander. No credit cards.

Train Bleu €€ *Gare de Lyon, 750012; tel: 01 43 43 09 06.* Open daily for lunch and dinner. Built over a century ago in the midst of the Gare de Lyon, this lavish-looking restaurant is considered an artistic marvel, with frescoed ceilings, mosaics and *belle époque* murals. Classic French dishes served quickly and efficiently. Major credit cards.

LEFT BANK (5–7, 14–15)

L'As du Fallafel € *34 rue des Rosiers, 75004; tel: 01 48 87 63 60.* Open Sun–Fri noon–midnight, closed Sat (Sabbath). The best *falafel* in Paris is a meal in itself. There are also *shawarma* sandwiches in pitta bread. Charming location in the heart of the Marais. Major credit cards.

Les Bookinistes €€ *53 quai des Grands Augustins, 75006; tel: 01 43 25 45 94.* Open weekdays for lunch and dinner; Sat dinner only. A modern bistro run by the inventive chef William Ledeuil, who has a gift for imaginative starters, fish tartars and polenta, pastas and salads. Ledeuil has opened another restaurant next door, Ze Kitchen Gallerie, with a menu of fish and vegetables cooked *a la plancha* (on a flat iron griddle). Major credit cards.

Jacques Cagna €€€€ *14 rue des Grands-Augustins, 75006; tel: 01 43 26 49 39.* Open weekdays for lunch and dinner; Sat dinner only. On the first floor of an old Parisian mansion on a quiet street close to St-Germain-des-Prés. Award-winning chef Jacques Cagna prepares the most imaginative dishes centred on fresh fish and seafood. Reservations are essential at least a week in advance. Major credit cards.

Casa Corsa €€ *25 rue Mazarine, 75006; tel: 01 44 07 38 98.* Open Tues–Sat for lunch and dinner, Mon lunch only. A culinary bastion of Corsica that does justice to its surprisingly diverse cuisine – from baby squid to braised veal. A lot of it is "peasant food fit for a king". The goat's cheese in walnut leaves is superb. Corsican wines by the glass. Major credit cards.

Chez Françoise €€ *Aérogare des Invalides, 75007; tel: 01 47 05 49 03.* Open daily for lunch and dinner. This bright and elegant restaurant is a favourite rendezvous for French parliamentarians. Pleasant terrace in summer and live jazz in the evening keeps the locals coming. Specialities include a langoustine salad with guacamole, roasted swordfish with candied green peppers, and coffee ice cream. Major credit cards.

Lipp €€ *151 blvd. St-Germain, 75006; tel: 01 45 48 53 91.* Open daily for lunch and dinner until 1am. Everyone who's anyone in St-Germain-des-Prés has a table here, and the place is filled with tourists, too. Not to be missed for a view of the neighbourhood eccentrics. Brasserie fare (Alsace country cooking), notably stews and *choucroute*. Reasonably priced house Riesling wine. Major credit cards.

Paul Minchelli €€€€ *54 blvd. de la Tour Maubourg, 75007; tel: 01 47 05 89 86.* Open Tues–Sat for lunch and dinner. This modern and cheerful Art Deco restaurant, named after its chef, has quickly acquired a name for some of the best seafood in Paris. The menu changes daily depending on the catch. The menu usually includes lobster, sea bass and tuna delicately prepared and beautifully served. Reservations are essential. Major credit cards.

Perraudin € *157 rue St-Jacques, 75005; tel: 01 46 33 15 75.* Open Tues–Fri for lunch and dinner, Sat–Mon dinner only. A favourite with students and budget travellers. Very inexpensive three-course meals and house wines. Serves a range of tasty country cooking in the Latin Quarter: *andouillette, boeuf bourguignon* and *tarte Tatin.* No credit cards.

Jules Verne €€€€ *2nd floor, Tour Eiffel, 75007; tel: 01 45 55 61 44.* Open daily for lunch and dinner. Offers a fine view of Paris, with cuisine and prices to match the altitude. Exciting modern decor by Slavik. The lobster fricassé and *escalope de foie gras* are the house specialities. Reserve several weeks in advance. Major credit cards.

INDEX